ICSNC 2018

The Thirteenth International Conference on Systems and Networks Communications

October 14 - 18, 2018

Nice, France

ICSNC 2018 Editors

Eugen Borcoci, University Politehnica of Bucarest, Romania

Przemyslaw Pochec University of New Brunswick Canada

Printed from e-media with permission by:

Curran Associates, Inc.
57 Morehouse Lane
Red Hook, NY 12571

Some format issues inherent in the e-media version may also appear in this print version.

Printed by Curran Associates, Inc. (2018)

International Academy, Research, and Industry Association (IARIA)
412 Derby Way
Wilmington, DE 19810

Phone: (408) 893-6407
Fax: (408) 527-6351

petre@iaria.org

Additional copies of this publication are available from:

Curran Associates, Inc.
57 Morehouse Lane
Red Hook, NY 12571 USA
Phone: 845-758-0400
Fax: 845-758-2633
Email: curran@proceedings.com
Web: www.proceedings.com

Table of Contents

ICSNC 2018

Forward

The Thirteenth International Conference on Systems and Networks Communications (ICSNC 2018), held on October 14 - 18, 2018- Nice, France, continued a series of events covering a broad spectrum of systems and networks related topics.

As a multi-track event, ICSNC 2018 served as a forum for researchers from the academia and the industry, professionals, standard developers, policy makers and practitioners to exchange ideas. The conference covered fundamentals on wireless, high-speed, mobile and Ad hoc networks, security, policy based systems and education systems. Topics targeted design, implementation, testing, use cases, tools, and lessons learnt for such networks and systems

The conference had the following tracks:

- TRENDS: Advanced features
- WINET: Wireless networks
- HSNET: High speed networks
- SENET: Sensor networks
- MHNET: Mobile and Ad hoc networks
- AP2PS: Advances in P2P Systems
- MESH: Advances in Mesh Networks
- VENET: Vehicular networks
- RFID: Radio-frequency identification systems
- SESYS: Security systems
- MCSYS: Multimedia communications systems
- POSYS: Policy-based systems
- PESYS: Pervasive education system

We welcomed technical papers presenting research and practical results, position papers addressing the pros and cons of specific proposals, such as those being discussed in the standard forums or in industry consortiums, survey papers addressing the key problems and solutions on any of the above topics, short papers on work in progress, and panel proposals.

We take here the opportunity to warmly thank all the members of the ICSNC 2018 technical program committee as well as the numerous reviewers. The creation of such a broad and high quality conference program would not have been possible without their involvement. We also kindly thank all the authors that dedicated much of their time and efforts to contribute to the ICSNC 2018. We truly believe that thanks to all these efforts, the final conference program consists of top quality contributions.

This event could also not have been a reality without the support of many individuals, organizations and sponsors. We also gratefully thank the members of the ICSNC 2018 organizing committee for their help in handling the logistics and for their work that is making this professional meeting a success. We gratefully appreciate to the technical program committee co-chairs that contributed to identify the appropriate groups to submit contributions.

We hope the ICSNC 2018 was a successful international forum for the exchange of ideas and results between academia and industry and to promote further progress in networking and systems communications research. We also hope Nice provided a pleasant environment during the conference and everyone saved some time for exploring this beautiful city.

ICSNC 2018 Steering Committee

Eugen Borcoci, University "Politehnica"of Bucharest (UPB), Romania
Sathiamoorthy Manoharan, University of Auckland, New Zealand
Leon Reznik, Rochester Institute of Technology, USA
Zoubir Mammeri, IRIT - Paul Sabatier University, Toulouse, France
Maiga Chang, Athabasca University, Canada
David Navarro, Lyon Institute of Nanotechnology, France
Christos Bouras, University of Patras / Computer Technology Institute & Press 'Diophantus', Greece

ICSNC 2018 Industry/Research Advisory Committee

Yasushi Kambayashi, Nippon Institute of Technology, Japan
Christopher Nguyen, Intel Corp., USA

ICSNC 2018

Committee

ICSNC Steering Committee

Eugen Borcoci, University "Politehnica"of Bucharest (UPB), Romania
Sathiamoorthy Manoharan, University of Auckland, New Zealand
Leon Reznik, Rochester Institute of Technology, USA
Zoubir Mammeri, IRIT - Paul Sabatier University, Toulouse, France
Maiga Chang, Athabasca University, Canada
David Navarro, Lyon Institute of Nanotechnology, France
Christos Bouras, University of Patras / Computer Technology Institute & Press 'Diophantus', Greece

ICSNC Industry/Research Advisory Committee

Yasushi Kambayashi, Nippon Institute of Technology, Japan
Christopher Nguyen, Intel Corp., USA

ICSNC 2018 Technical Program Committee

Habtamu Abie, Norwegian Computing Center - Oslo, Norway
Talal Alharbi, University of Queensland, Australia
G. G. Md. Nawaz Ali, Nanyang Technological University (NTU), Singapore
Samr Samir Ali, Abu Dhabi University, UAE
Muhammad Sohaib Ayub, Lahore University of Management Sciences (LUMS), Pakistan
K. Hari Babu, Birla Institute of Technology & Science (BITS Pilani), India
Ilija Basicevic, University of Novi Sad, Serbia
Robert Bestak, Czech Technical University in Prague, Czech Republic
Eugen Borcoci, University "Politehnica"of Bucharest (UPB), Romania
Christos Bouras, University of Patras / Computer Technology Institute & Press <Diophantus>, Greece
An Braeken, Vrije Universiteit Brussel, Belgium
Martin Brandl, Danube University Krems, Austria
Francesco Buccafurri, University of Reggio Calabria, Italy
Dumitru Dan Burdescu, University of Craiova, Romania
Vicente Casares Giner, Universitat Politècnica de València, Spain
Maiga Chang, Athabasca University, Canada
Hao Che, University of Texas at Arlington, USA
Stefano Chessa, University of Pisa, Italy
Enrique Chirivella, University of the West of Scotland, UK
Jorge A. Cobb, The University of Texas at Dallas, USA
Bernard Cousin, Irisa | University of Rennes 1, France
Fisnik Dalipi, University College of Southeast Norway, Norway
Sima Das, MST, USA
Poonam Dharam, Saginaw Valley State University, USA
Gulustan Dogan, Yildiz Technical University, Istanbul, Turkey
Jawad Drissi, Cameron University, USA

Safwan El Assad, University of Nantes, France
Marco Furini, University of Modena and Reggio Emilia, Italy
Katja Gilly, Universidad Miguel Hernández, Spain
Hector Marco Gisbert, University of the West of Scotland, UK
Rich Groves, A10 Networks, USA
Anna Guerra, University of Bologna, Italy
Barbara Guidi, University of Pisa, Italy
Youcef Hammal, USTHB University Bab-Ezzouar, Algeria
Eman Hammad, University of Toronto, Canada
Chitra Javali, UNSW Sydney, Australia
Muhammad Javed, Cameron University, USA
Fang-zhou Jiang, Data61 | CSIRO & UNSW, Australia
Yasushi Kambayashi, Nippon Institute of Technology, Japan
Sarah Kamel, Télécom ParisTech, France
Sokratis K. Katsikas, Norwegian University of Science & Technology (NTNU), Norway
Jinoh Kim, Texas A&M University-Commerce, USA
Yagmur Kirkagac, Netas Telecommunication Inc., Turkey
Peng-Yong Kong, Khalifa University, United Arab Emirates
Michał Król, University College London, UK
Takashi Kurimoto, National Institute of Informatics, Japan
Gyu Myoung Lee, Liverpool John Moores University, UK
Jin-Shyan Lee, National Taipei University of Technology (TAIPEI TECH), Taiwan
Shunbo Lei, University of Hong Kong, Hong Kong
Wolfgang Leister, Norsk Regnesentral (Norwegian Computing Center), Norway
Shouxi Luo, Southwest Jiaotong University, China
Zoubir Mammeri, IRIT - Paul Sabatier University, Toulouse, France
Sathiamoorthy Manoharan, University of Auckland, New Zealand
Francisco J. Martinez, University of Zaragoza, Spain
Victor Mehmeri, Technical University of Denmark (DTU), Denmark
Farouk Mezghani, Inria Lille - Nord Europe, France
David Navarro, Lyon Institute of Nanotechnology, France
Christopher Nguyen, Intel Corp., USA
António Nogueira, University of Aveiro / Instituto de Telecomunicações, Portugal
Jun Peng, University of Texas - Rio Grande Valley, USA
Zeeshan Pervez, University of the West of Scotland, UK
Kandaraj Piamrat, LS2N | University of Nantes, France
Paulo Pinto, Universidade Nova de Lisboa, Portugal
Aneta Poniszewska, Lodz University of Technology, Poland
Victor Ramos, Metropolitan Autonomous University, Mexico
Piotr Remlein, Poznan University of Technology, Poland
Yongmao Ren, Chinese Academy of Sciences, China
Leon Reznik, Rochester Institute of Technology, USA
Mohsen Rezvani, Shahrood University of Technology, Iran
Sebastian Rieger, Fulda University of Applied Sciences, Germany
Laborde Romain, University Paul Sabatier (Toulouse 3), France
Imed Romdhani, Edinburgh Napier University, UK
Luis Enrique Sánchez Crespo, University of Castilla-la Mancha & Sicaman Nuevas Tecnologías Ciudad Real, Spain

Copyright Information

M2ANET Performance under Multiple Competing Data Flows

Oluwatola Ayansiji, John DeDourek, Przemyslaw Pochec
Faculty of Computer Science
University of New Brunswick
Fredericton, Canada
e-mail: { tola.ayansiji, dedourek, pochec}@unb.ca

Abstract—**A Mobile Ad hoc Network (MANET) is a network of wireless mobile devices capable of communicating with one another without any reliance on a fixed infrastructure. A Mobile Medium Ad hoc Network (M2ANET) is a set of mobile forwarding nodes functioning as relays for facilitating communication between the users of this Mobile Medium. The performance of a Mobile Medium depends not only on the forwarding node density, their distribution and movement but also is affected by the traffic load present in the Medium. The traffic in the Mobile Medium may be due to multiple users using the Medium or due to rogue users performing a Denial of Service (DOS) attack. We investigate the performance of a Mobile Medium serving multiple users under different routing protocols, focusing on the performance of the Ad hoc On-demand Distance Vector (AODV) routing protocol. The simulation results show that the packet delivery is only moderately affected (Packet Delivery Ratio (PDR) dropped form 93% to 83% in the sample network) by the presence of a competing flow in the Medium, due to the resilience of ad hoc networks. On the other hand, in the same network, the packet delay is affected significantly (four fold increase in packet delay, from 0.2s to 0.8s, in the sample network).**

Keywords-MANET; M2ANET; performance; delivery ratio; delay; multiple data flows; DOS.

I. INTRODUCTION

A MANET is a set of mobile devices that cooperate with each other by exchanging messages and forwarding data [1]. A Mobile Medium Ad hoc Network (M2ANET) proposed in [2] is a particular configuration of a typical MANET where all mobile nodes are divided into two categories: (i) the forwarding only nodes forming the so called Mobile Medium, and (ii) the communicating nodes, mobile or otherwise, that send data and use this Mobile Medium for communication. The advantage of this M2ANET model is that the performance of such a network is based on how well the Mobile Medium can carry the messages between the communicating nodes and not based on whether all mobile nodes form a fully connected network. An example of a M2ANET is a cloud of autonomous drones released over an area of interest facilitating communication in this area. The movement of nodes in a M2ANET can be preplanned by the user, selected at random or purposefully controlled for the best network performance. When the mobile nodes are designed to guide their movement themselves, we call such a network a Self-organizing Mobile Medium Ad hoc Network (SMMANET) [3].

As in any network, the performance depends on many factors: link data rates, protocol used and, for MANET type networks, node density and movement pattern. The traffic pattern and network congestion will also have an impact on M2ANET performance. In this paper, we set out to investigate the effect of additional users on M2ANET performance. These new users can be legitimate users of the M2ANET or even some rogue nodes purposely interfering with legitimate M2ANET operations.

In Section II, we present background on M2ANETs and their operation. The simulation experiment investigating the presence of multiple flows in a M2ANET on its performance is presented in Section III, with results analyzed in Section IV. The conclusion is in Section V.

II. STATE OF THE ART

We introduced the concept of a Mobile Medium in our seminal paper on M2ANETS in 2011 [2]. A M2ANET realizes the connection between two hosts with the cloud of nodes serving as the data communication medium (aka Mobile Medium) and forming the communication channel. Any particular connection in the Medium does not matter as long as the channel between communicating users of the M2ANET can be formed. As a consequence, M2ANETs exhibit fault-resilience, given that they are not operating with a single point of failure. Examples of networks operating on a similar principle include the Google Loon project [4], Facebook's flying internet service [5] and a swarming micro air vehicle network (SMAVNET II) [6].

Despite the possibility that the nodes forming a Mobile Medium can operate in a manner similar to traditional MANETS using the same type of hardware nodes and the same routing protocols, the means of investigation of M2ANETs are different from traditional approaches to investigating ad hoc networks as they rely on different performance metrics. Specifically, the performance of any individual links and the connectivity between the M2ANET nodes does not matter directly. What is important is the performance of the channel through the Mobile Medium allowing the users of the M2ANET to communicate successfully. For example, the question whether all the nodes in the Mobile Medium are connected together is of no importance.

Our past investigation of M2ANETs centered on the following issues: node density in the Mobile Medium, node movement pattern and the cooperation among the nodes.

The node density in general indicates how many mobile forwarding nodes are present in an area of interest where wireless communication is to be supported by means of the Mobile Medium. The smaller the area and the larger the number nodes the better the performance that the M2ANET offered to the users of the Medium [2]. For a M2ANET to operate efficiently, the available mobile nodes need to be positioned and moved over the area of coverage. Having the forwarding nodes mobile contributes to greater resiliency of the implementation, because new nodes move in and take over form the failing ones [7], and allows for the use of aerial drones, like micro air vehicles/planes [6], with hard limits on the sustained minimum velocity. M2ANET mobile nodes can move at random [8], in groups [9], along fractal paths [10] or can even be cooperating among themselves like an intelligent swarm, to best facilitate the demand from M2ANET users [3].

Our past investigations of M2ANETs focused on the Mobile Medium operating autonomously and serving a pair of users, similar to having two users connecting wirelessly with a line of sight link. In this paper, we set out to investigate the behavior of the Mobile Medium in the presence of multiple data flows being carried simultaneously in a M2ANET. There are many practical scenarios that correspond to this model: (i) a simple scenario where multiple users rely on the same Mobile Medium to carry their data and (ii) a malicious attack scenario, where rogue nodes inject data into the Mobile Medium in an attempt to interfere with the legitimate traffic.

III. PERFORMANCE OF A M2ANET IN THE PRESENCE OF COMPETING FLOWS

The performance of the Mobile Medium in the presence of competing flow is investigated using the ns2 simulator [11] in a simulated generic scenario with a preset number of Mobile Medium nodes moving randomly in a bounded region. As in the previous studies [2][3][7]-[10], the performance of the Mobile Medium is measured at different forwarding node densities by varying the number of nodes in the M2ANET network. Experiments with three different MANET routing protocols: AODV, Destination Sequenced Distance Vector (DSDV), and Dynamic Source Routing (DSR) are conducted [12]. Three user scenarios are investigated: a pair of users communicated through the Mobile Medium without any other traffic present (so called "no DOS" scenario), and the same but with one or two other flows active across the Medium (DOS1 and DOS2 scenarios). In the multi flow scenarios, the additional flows, for the sake of argument, are considered as rogue flows that are interfering with the original flow (thus the name DOS1/2: Denial Of Service with one/two rogue flow(s) scenario) and only the performance of the first (principal) flow is investigated. In order to investigate the potential interference between data flows in the Mobile Medium, the locations of the sources and destinations were selected so that straight line paths between pairs of users would intersect with one another, Figure 1.

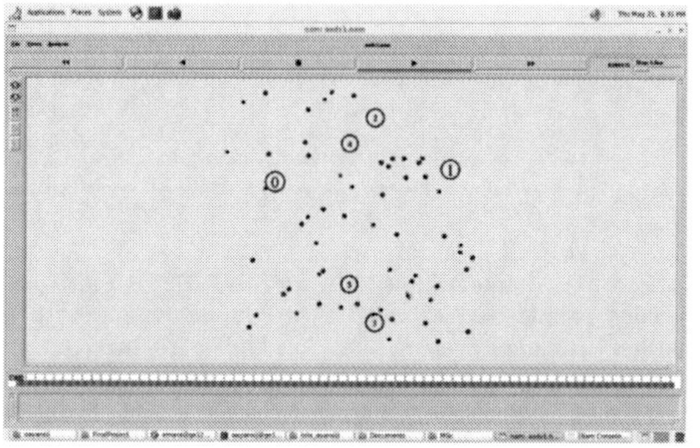

Figure 1. Screen shot of the simulation showing a M2ANET network with two communicating nodes 0 and 1, and four rogue nodes 2 to 5.

In the mobile network simulation, the random mobility model is used as a reference case scenario, mostly because it is a standard model used in network simulation. The base case model used is the Random Way Point (RWP) model available in ns2 [11]. In RWP, nodes are moved in a piecewise linear fashion, with each linear segment pointing to a randomly selected destination and the node moving at a constant, but randomly selected speed. The mobile nodes forming the Mobile Medium move at random speeds with an average speed of 4 m/s. The main communicating nodes 0 and 1 are stationary. The source and destination nodes are located at (200,650) and (900,700) coordinates, respectively. The simulation details are summarized in Table 1.

TABLE I. SIMULATION PARAMETERS

Parameters	
Simulator	NS-2.34
Channel Type	Channel / Wireless Channel
Network Interface Type	Phy/WirelessPhy
Mac Type	Mac/802.11
Radio-Propagation Type	Propagation/Two-ray ground
Interface Queue Type	Queue/Drop Tail
Link Layer Type	LL
Antenna	Antenna/Omni Antenna
Maximum Packets in ifq	50
Area (n * n)	1000 x 1000m
Source Type	CBR over UDP packetSize_ 512 interval_ 0.05
Simulation Time	300 s
Routing Protocol	AODV, DSDV, DSR

The data traffic for each flow is modelled with the CBR traffic generator and sent using UDP over simulated Mobile Medium networks with five different node densities from 20 to 120 nodes. Node density indicates the total number of mobile nodes in the 1000 m by 1000 m square region modelled in the experiments. The delivery ratio is the ratio of the number of packets successfully received at the destination node to the number of packets sent during each simulation experiment. The packet delivery time (delay) is the difference between the time the packet was received at the destination and the time the same packet was sent from the source node. Each mobile network scenario has been simulated three times for a 300 second simulation run time and the average results taken.

IV. Results and Analysis

The Mobile Medium performed as expected (matching the packet delivery rate results of previous studies, e.g., [2]) when presented with a single flow to transmit and no other flows interfering with it, i.e., no DOS. When additional flows were present in the Mobile Medium the performance decreased. The decrease was more pronounced for DSDV and DSR, and very moderate for AODV, in the presence of moderate disturbance to the Mobile Medium (only one additional rogue flow in DOS1), Figure 2. Better performance of AODV can be attributed to it being reactive and distributed [1][12].

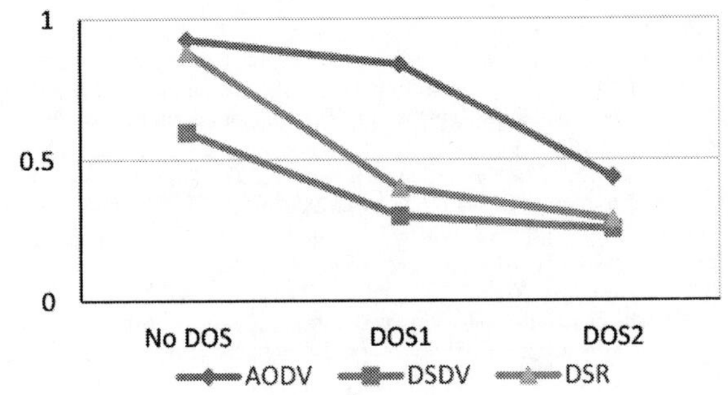

Figure 2. Delivery ratio for three scenarios.

Further investigation of the DOS1 scenario shows that the AODV advantage is present over the full range of node densities, Figure 3 and 4. Finally, with more significant load in the Mobile Medium, i.e., in the presence of two rogue flows in DOS2, the delivery ratio for all tested routing protocols dropped similarly to just below 50%, as seen in Figure 2.

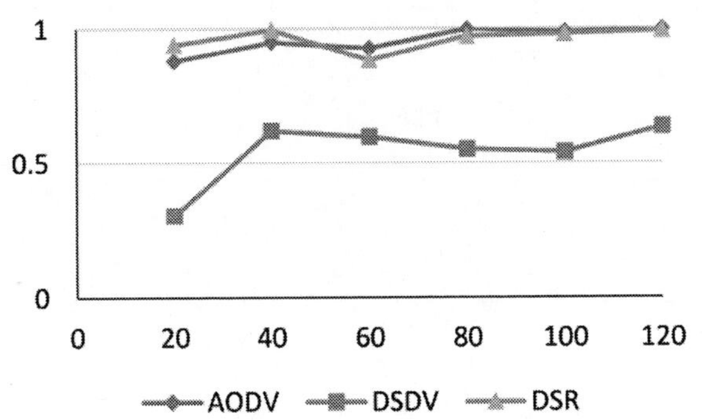

Figure 3. Packet delivery ratio vs number of nodes, no DOS.

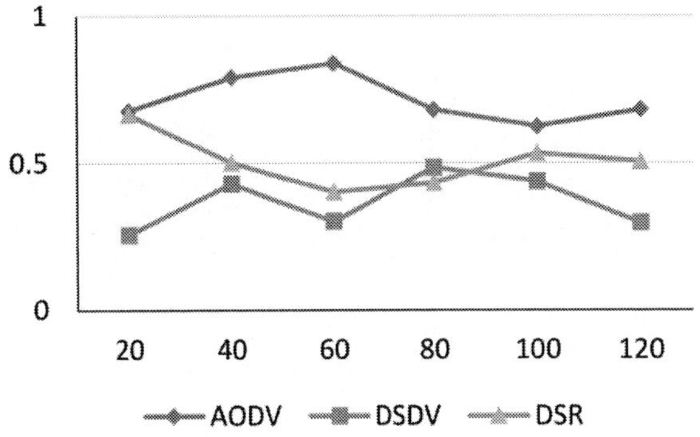

Figure 4. Packet delivery ratio vs number of nodes, DOS1.

The investigation of packet delivery times shows significant increases in the average packet delays when a second flow is present, DOS1 scenario. In the single flow scenario, no DOS, the delays were well below 0.5s in all experiments across all node densities, Figure 5. With the second flow present, the DOS1 scenario, the delays increased in general, with the most significant delay in the range of 5s registered in the DSR experiments, Figure 6. For the best performing protocol, AODV, the delays were below 0.2s in the single flow scenario and up to 0.79s in the DOS1 scenario.

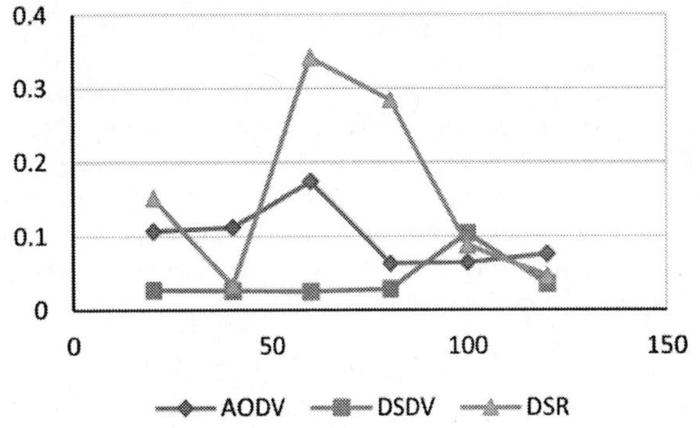

Figure 5. Average delay [sec] vs number of nodes, no DOS.

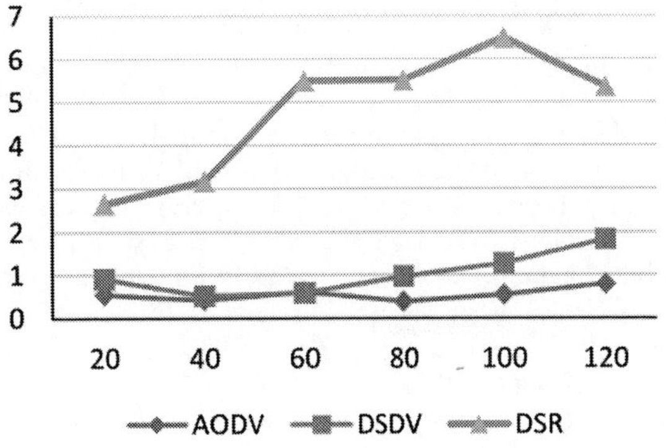

Figure 6. Average delay [sec] vs number of nodes, DOS1.

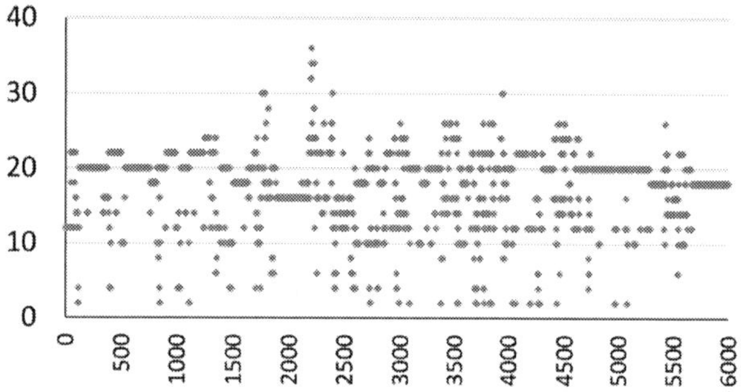

Figure 7. AODV: path lenght for each packet sent, DOS1.

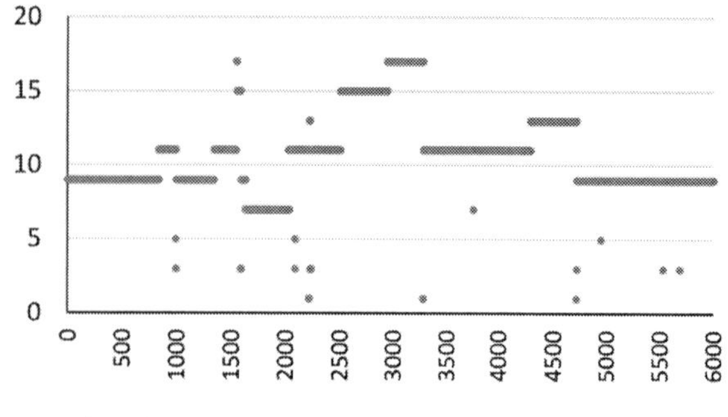

Figure 8. AODV: path lenght for each packet sent, no DOS.

Further investigation of the AODV protocol indicates that increase in packet delays may be attributed to much longer forwarding path lengths, and more frequent path changes. In the network with two flows, DOS1, up to 34 hops were registered for packet 2200 on Figure 7, compared to the path length reaching only 17 in a network with a single flow, no DOS scenario in Figure 8.

V. Conclusion and Future Work

Previous studies showed the dependence of the performance of a Mobile Medium on network infrastructure characteristics: the forwarding node density, movement pattern, routing protocol etc. In this paper, we showed how the Mobile Medium performance is affected by the presence of multiple flows in the network. Introducing competing flows in the Mobile Medium network results in gradual degradation of packet delivery ratio, from close to 93% for AODV for a single flow scenario, down to 83% for two flows and only 44% for three flows. The decrease is even more significant for DSDV and DSR. What is more significant, the Mobile Medium experiences a drastic increase in average packet delays when the second flow is added across all investigated configurations. The AODV average delays increased from less than 0.2s up to 0.79s. The delays for the worst performing DSR increased from 0.79s to 6.48s.

The Mobile Medium, while showing a great resilience to packet loss with a moderate traffic increase, is expected to experience significant delays in packet delivery when the traffic carried through the medium increases.

Future work could focus on investigation of AODV class routing protocols (on-demand, reactive) centering on maintaining high delivery ratio while improving on packet delays.

References

[1] S. Basagni, M. Conti, S. Giordano, and I. Stojmenovic (Eds.), Mobile Ad Hoc Networking, New York, Wiley-IEEE Press, 2001.

[2] J. DeDourek and P. Pochec, "M2ANET: a Mobile Medium Ad Hoc Network", Wireless Sensor Networks: Theory and Practice, WSN 2011, Paris, France, Feb. 2011, pp. 1-4.

[3] H. Almutairi, J. DeDourek, and P. Pochec, "Node Movement Control Based on Swarm Intelligence for a Mobile Medium Ad hoc Network", The Eight International Conference on Advances in Future Internet, AFIN2016, July 27, 2016, Nice, France, pp. 1-8.

[4] H. Hodson, "Google's Project Loon to float the internet on balloons", New Scientist, October 2013.

[5] J. Brustein, "Facebook's Flying Internet Service, Brought to You by Drones", Bloomberg Businessweek, March 4, 2014.

[6] A. J. Pacheco, et al., "Implementation of a Wireless Mesh Network of Ultra Light MAVs with Dynamic Routing; Proceedings of the IEEE Globe Work; Anaheim, CA, USA. 3–7 December 2012, pp. 1591–1596

[7] K. Patel, J. DeDourek, and P. Pochec, "M2ANET Performance Under Variable Node Sleep Times", Third International Conference on Advances in Future Internet, AFIN2011, Nice, France, Aug. 2011, pp. 31-34.

[8] M. Alzaylaee, J. DeDourek, and P. Pochec, "Linear Node Movement Patterns in MANETS", The Ninth International Conference on Wireless and Mobile Communications ICWMC 2013, Nice, France, July 21-26, 2013, pp. 162-166.

[9] A. Alshehri, J. DeDourek, and P. Pochec, "The Advantage of Moving Nodes in Formations in MANETs and M2ANETs", The Ninth International Conference on Wireless and Mobile Communications ICWMC 2013, Nice, France, July 21-26, 2013, pp. 228-232.

[10] H. Alseef, J. DeDourek, and P. Pochec, "A Method for Custom Movement Generation in Wireless Mobile Network Simulation", The Seventh International Conference on Emerging Networks and Systems Intelligence, EMERGING 2015, July 19 - 24, 2015, Nice, France, pp. 27-32.

[11] H. Ekram and T. Issariyakul, Introduction to Network Simulator ns2, Springer, 2009

[12] S. K. Sarkar, T. G. Basavaraju, and C. Puttamadappa, Ad Hoc Mobile Wireless Networks, Principles, Protocols, and Applications, Auerbach Publications Taylor & Francis Group, 2007.

An Efficient Estimation Scheme of Timing Offset for OFDM Transmission Over Multipath Fading Channels

Keunhong Chae, Eunyoung Cho, and Seokho Yoon
College of Information and Communication Engineering
Sungkyunkwan University
Suwon, South Korea
e-mail: syoon@skku.edu

Abstract— **This paper proposes a novel estimation scheme of the timing offset for orthogonal frequency division multiplexing transmission over multipath fading channels. We first design an impulse-like correlation function and obtain the sample standard deviation of the correlation values, and then, develop a decision metric based on the reciprocals of the sample standard deviations for the timing offset estimation, which has the maximum value when the timing offset is estimated correctly. Unlike the conventional schemes, the proposed scheme exploits the change in statistics by the first-arriving path rather than the magnitude itself of the first-arriving path. Numerical results show that the proposed timing offset estimation scheme offers a performance improvement over the conventional schemes in various multipath fading channels.**

Keywords- OFDM; timing offset estimation; multipath fading channels; decision metric; standard deviation

I. INTRODUCTION AND RELATED WORKS

Compared with the single carrier communication systems, Orthogonal Frequency Division Multiplexing (OFDM) has many advantages such as simple equalization and high spectral efficiency [1]. However, the OFDM is very sensitive to the timing synchronization error [2]: Specifically, the timing offset causes an error in determining the starting point of the Fast Fourier Transform (FFT) window at the receiver, eventually resulting in a serious Signal-to-Noise Ratio (SNR) degradation [1]. Although several timing offset estimation techniques [3]-[7] were proposed, all of them do not perform well under the influence of the multipath fading common in wireless channels, since they often mistake one of the timings of the delayed paths for the (correct) timing of the first-arriving path, i.e., they suffer from a problem of ambiguity in timing. Thus, the timing offset estimation techniques alleviating the influence of the multipath fading were developed: [8] takes the earliest among the paths with magnitudes exceeding a pre-determined threshold as the first-arriving path, and on the other hand, [9] and [10] perform a preprocessing based on power normalization to increase the relative magnitude of the first-arriving path to those of the delayed paths. Although these techniques offer an improvement in timing offset estimation to some degree, all of them would perform poorly when the first-arriving path is attenuated severely or when the first-arriving path is not the strongest one.

In this paper, thus, we propose a novel timing offset estimation scheme with a higher degree of robustness to the multipath fading, where we exploit the change in statistics by the first-arriving path rather than the magnitude itself of the first-arriving path, unlike in the conventional schemes. Specifically, we estimate the timing offset based on the change in the reciprocal of the standard deviation of the correlation samples of the OFDM symbol. From numerical results, the proposed scheme is confirmed to provide a better estimation performance over the conventional schemes in multipath fading environments.

In the following sections, we describe the OFDM system model in multipath channel environments (Section II), propose a novel timing offset estimation scheme (Section III), compare the performance of the proposed and conventional schemes (Section IV), and finally, conclude this paper with a brief summary (Section V).

II. SYSTEM MODEL

The baseband equivalent of the n-th received OFDM sample $y(n)$ can be expressed as

$$y(n)=\sum_{l=0}^{L-1} m(l)s(n-\varepsilon-l)e^{j2\pi\Delta f n/N}+w(n), \qquad (1)$$

where $\{s(n)\}_{n=-N_p}^{N-1}$ is a transmitted OFDM signal comprising the data part $\{s(n)\}_{n=0}^{N-1}$ with size N and the Cyclic Prefix (CP) part $\{s(n)\}_{n=-N_p}^{-1}$ with size N_p, ε is the timing offset normalized to the sample interval, Δf is the carrier frequency offset normalized to the subcarrier spacing $1/N$, $m(l)$ is the l-th channel coefficient of a multipath fading channel with length L, and $w(n)$ is the complex Gaussian noise sample with mean zero and variance $\sigma_w^2=E[|w(n)|^2]$, where $E[\cdot]$ denotes the statistical expectation. In this paper, we consider the timing offset estimation based on training symbols and it is assumed that a training symbol $\{s(n)\}_{n=0}^{N-1}$ with two identical halves (i.e., $s(n)=s(n+N/2)$ for $n=0,1,\cdots,N/2-1$) is used, as in other studies.

III. PROPOSED SCHEME

A. Generation of Impulse-like Correlation Function

Considering that the ideal form of the correlation function for the timing offset estimation is the impulse-like

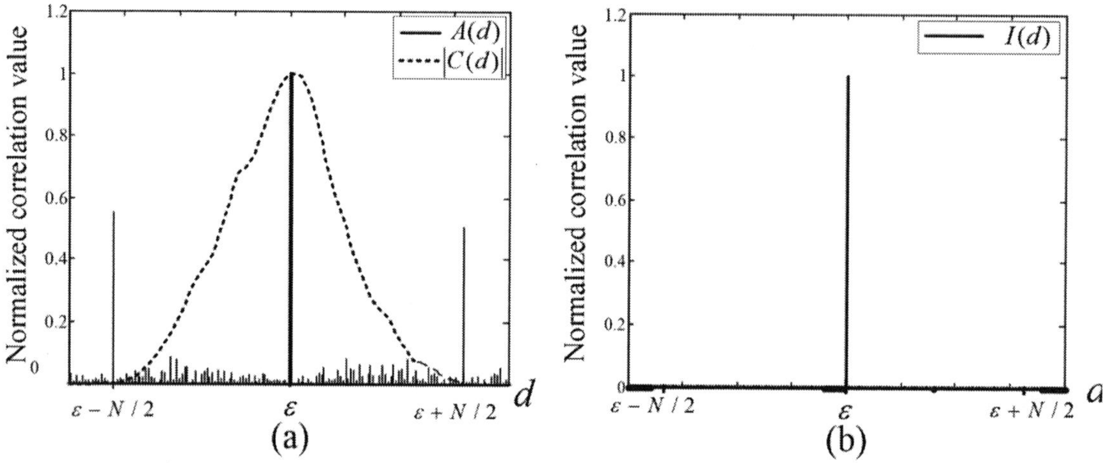

Figure 1. (a) $A(d)$ and $|C(d)|$ in the absence of channel distortion. (b) $I(d)$ in the absence of channel distortion.

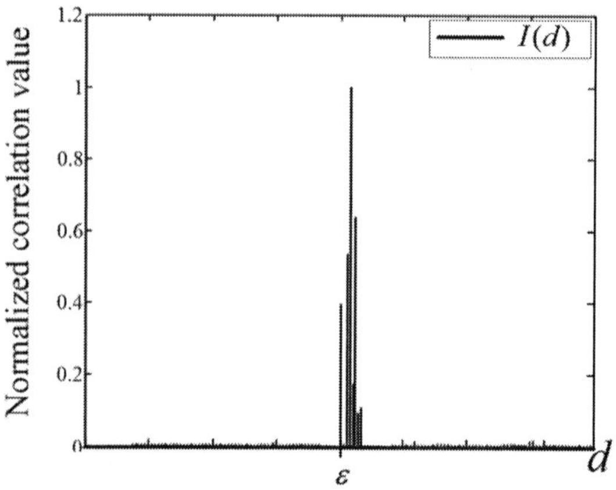

Figure 2. $I(d)$ in a multipath Rayleigh fading channel with an 8-path exponential power delay profile.

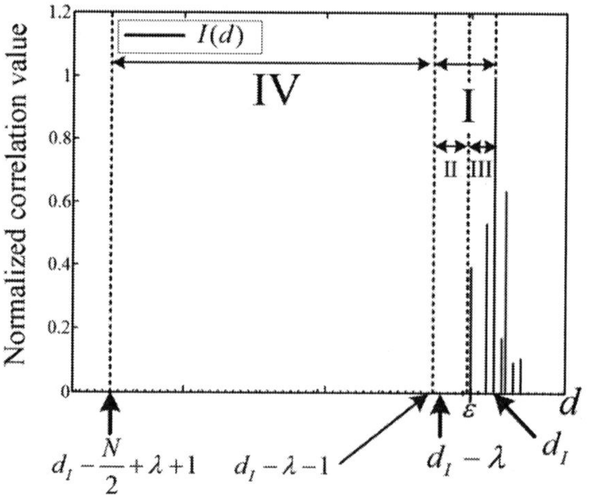

Figure 3. A magnified version of Figure 2.

one, where the correlation is very high at the correct timing, whereas the correlation remains very low at the incorrect timings, we first generate

$$A(d)=\sum_{k=0}^{N-1} y(d+k)s^{*}(k) \tag{2}$$

by correlating the received OFDM samples and a locally generated training symbol samples, where d is the candidate for the timing offset ε. As shown in Figure 1(a), $A(d)$ has three correlation peaks at $d=\varepsilon$ and $\varepsilon \pm (N/2)$, and the two correlation peaks at $\varepsilon \pm (N/2)$ can be significantly reduced by the product of $|A(d)|^2$ and

$$C(d)=\frac{1}{N_P+1}\sum_{i=0}^{N_P}\left|\sum_{k=0}^{N/2-1} y^{*}(d-i+k)y(d-i+k+N/2)\right|^2 \tag{3}$$

with $(\bullet)^{*}$ the complex conjugate operation, as shown in Figure 1(b), where

$$I(d)=|A(d)|^2 \cdot C(d) \tag{4}$$

and it should be noted that $C(d)$ is the moving average of the absolute-squared correlation between the received OFDM samples with length $N/2$. Although $I(d)$ has an impulse-like form, it is severely distorted by multipath fading as shown in Figure 2, where the multipath channel is assumed to be Rayleigh distributed with an 8-path exponential Power Delay Profile (PDP). Yet, we will propose a novel timing offset estimation scheme exploiting the distorted $I(d)$, since it still keeps its impulse-like feature to some degree.

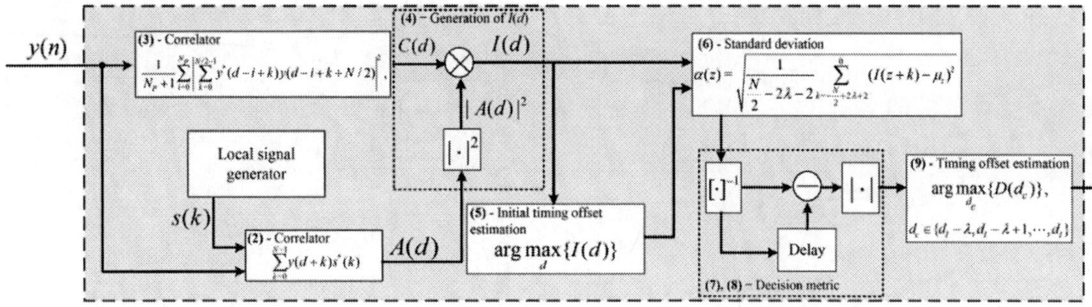

Figure 4. The overall structure of the proposed timing estimator.

B. Proposed Timing Offset Estimation Scheme

Using $I(d)$, first, we obtain an initial timing offset estimate d_I as

$$d_I = \arg\max_d \{I(d)\}. \quad (5)$$

From Figure 3, then, we can expect that $I(\varepsilon)$ would be within the interval I ($d_I - \lambda \le d \le d_I$), where λ is such that all channel paths are expected to be received within $\lambda+1$ samples (i.e., $\lambda \in \{L-1, L, \cdots, N_P\}$). Denoting d in the interval I by d_c (i.e., $d_c \in \{d_I-\lambda, d_I-\lambda+1, \cdots, d_I\}$), thus, we can make the following three observations: (i) The values of $I(d_c)$ in the sub-interval II ($d_I - \lambda \le d_c \le \varepsilon - 1$) are much smaller than those in the sub-interval III ($\varepsilon \le d_c \le d_I$), (ii) the values of $I(d)$ in the sub-interval IV ($d_I - N/2 + \lambda + 1 \le d \le d_I - \lambda - 1$) have statistics similar to those of the values of $I(d_c)$ in the sub-interval II, but different from those of the values of $I(d_c)$ in the sub-interval III, and (iii) the timing offset ε is the smallest value of d_c in the sub-interval III. Based on the observations, now, we can model the estimating problem of the timing offset as the detecting problem of the variation between the values of $I(d)$ for $d_I - N/2 + \lambda + 1 \le d \le \varepsilon - 1$ and those of $I(d)$ for $\varepsilon \le d \le d_I$, and we exploit the sample standard deviation

$$\alpha(z) = \sqrt{\frac{1}{\frac{N}{2} - 2\lambda - 2} \sum_{k=-\frac{N}{2}+2\lambda+2}^{0} (I(z+k) - \mu_z)^2}, \quad (6)$$

of $I(d)$ for $z \in \{d_I - \lambda - 1, d_I - \lambda, \cdots, d_I\}$ as a measure for detecting the variation, where μ_z is the sample mean of $I(d)$ for $z - \frac{N}{2} + 2\lambda + 2 \le d \le z$. It should be noted that the standard deviation is more sensitive to the variation of $I(d)$ compared with the variance, due to it being expressed in the same unit as that of $I(d)$, and thus, the standard deviation would offer a better performance in detecting the variation over the variance. Since ε is the smallest value of d_c in the sub-interval III and $I(d_c)$ in the sub-interval III often varies significantly, $|\alpha(\varepsilon) - \alpha(\varepsilon-1)|$ is expected to be larger than $|\alpha(d_c) - \alpha(d_c - 1)|$ in the sub-interval II, whereas to be smaller than $|\alpha(d_c) - \alpha(d_c-1)|$ in the sub-interval III. In this paper, we thus propose to use

$$D(d_c) = \left| \frac{1}{\alpha(d_c)} - \frac{1}{\alpha(d_c-1)} \right| = \left| \frac{\alpha(d_c-1) - \alpha(d_c)}{\alpha(d_c)\alpha(d_c-1)} \right| \quad (7)$$

as the decision metric for detecting the variation for $d_c \in \{d_I-\lambda, d_I-\lambda+1, \cdots, d_I\}$. Unlike $|\alpha(d_c) - \alpha(d_c-1)|$, $D(d_c)$ has its maximum value at $d_c = \varepsilon$ as shown in the following: (i) $\alpha(d_c) \cong \alpha(d_c-1)$ when $d_c < \varepsilon$, and thus, $D(d_c) \cong \left| \frac{0}{\alpha(d_c)\alpha(d_c-1)} \right| = 0$ (ii) $\alpha(\varepsilon) \gg \alpha(\varepsilon-1)$ when $d_c = \varepsilon$, and thus, $D(\varepsilon) \cong \left| -\frac{\alpha(\varepsilon)}{\alpha(\varepsilon)\alpha(\varepsilon-1)} \right| = \frac{1}{\alpha(\varepsilon-1)}$, and (iii) $\alpha(d_c) \gg \alpha(\varepsilon-1)$ and $\alpha(d_c-1) \gg \alpha(\varepsilon-1)$ when $d_c > \varepsilon$, and thus, $D(d_c) = \left| \frac{1}{\alpha(d_c)} - \frac{1}{\alpha(d_c-1)} \right| < \frac{1}{\alpha(\varepsilon-1)} = D(\varepsilon)$. The discussions above can be summarized as

$$D(d_c) = \begin{cases} \left| \frac{\alpha(d_c-1) - \alpha(d_c)}{\alpha(d_c)\alpha(d_c-1)} \right| \cong 0, & \text{when } d_c < \varepsilon, \\ \left| \frac{\alpha(d_c-1) - \alpha(d_c)}{\alpha(d_c)\alpha(d_c-1)} \right| \cong \frac{1}{\alpha(\varepsilon-1)}, & \text{when } d_c = \varepsilon, \\ \left| \frac{1}{\alpha(d_c)} - \frac{1}{\alpha(d_c-1)} \right| < \frac{1}{\alpha(\varepsilon-1)}, & \text{when } d_c > \varepsilon, \end{cases} \quad (8)$$

for $d_c \in \{d_I-\lambda, d_I-\lambda+1, \cdots, d_I\}$, where we can see that $D(d_c)$ has the maximum value when $d_c = \varepsilon$ regardless of the multipath components, and thus, the proposed scheme is anticipated to achieve the robustness to the channel attenuation and randomness. Finally, we can obtain the timing offset estimate

$$\hat{\varepsilon} = \arg\max_{d_c} \{D(d_c)\} \quad (9)$$

for $d_c \in \{d_I-\lambda, d_I-\lambda+1, \cdots, d_I\}$. Figure 4 depicts the structure of the proposed timing estimator comprising the operations in (2)-(9).

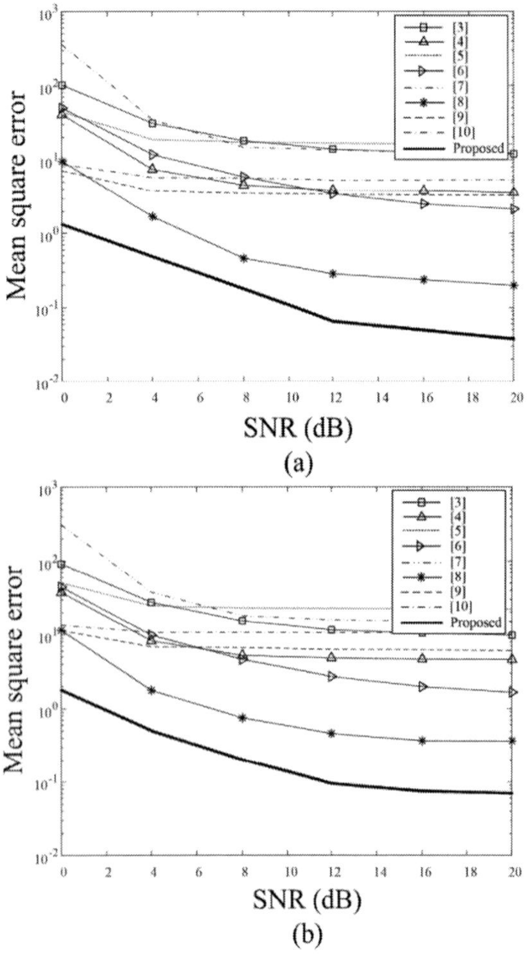

Figure 5. The MSE performances of the timing offset estimation schemes in an 8-path multipath fading channel with (a) exponential power delay profile (E-PDP) and (b) uniform power delay profile (U-PDP).

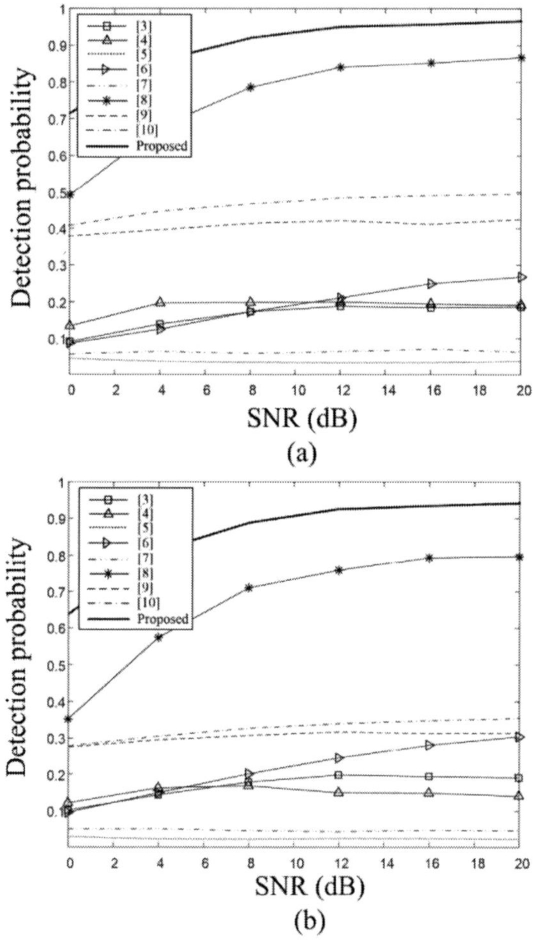

Figure 6. The detection probabilities of the timing offset estimation schemes in an 8-path multipath fading channel with (a) exponential power delay profile (E-PDP) and (b) uniform power delay profile (U-PDP).

IV. NUMERICAL RESULTS

In this section, the timing offset estimation performance of the proposed scheme is compared with those of the conventional schemes in [3]-[10] in terms of the Mean Square Error (MSE) and detection probability in multipath fading environments. We assume the following real transmission parameters: The IFFT size $N = 128$, the CP length $N_P = 8$, the carrier frequency offset $\Delta f = 0.1$, and 8-path multipath Rayleigh fading channels with exponential (E-) and uniform (U-) PDPs having the average power of $e^{-l/8}/\{\sum_{l=0}^{7} e^{-l/8}\}$ and $1/8$, respectively. In addition, the probability of false alarm and λ are set to 10^{-5} and N_P, respectively.

From Figure 5 showing the MSE and detection performances of the timing offset estimation schemes as a function of the SNR defined as $E[|s(k)|^2]/\sigma_w^2$ over the multipath fading channels, we can clearly see that the proposed scheme provides a better performance in timing estimation over the conventional schemes as expected. Especially, from the figures, it is observed that the difference in performance is more significant with the E-PDP than with the U-PDP of the multipaths, which stems from the fact that the variation in statistics by the first-arriving path is more pronounced compared with those of the delayed paths with the E-PDP than with the U-PDP of the multipaths, and thus, the advantage of the proposed scheme based on the change in statistics by the first-arriving path is more prominent with E-PDP over the conventional schemes based on the magnitude itself of the first-arriving path. In addition, the difference in performance increases as the value of SNR becomes larger. This is because the influence of the multipaths becomes more dominant over the noise in high SNR region, and thus, the advantage of the proposed scheme (designed to alleviate the influence of the multipaths) becomes more obvious than it is in low SNR region.

In short, we can conclude that the proposed scheme overcomes the multipath fading more efficiently than the conventional schemes.

V. Conclusion

In this paper, we have proposed a novel timing offset estimation scheme for OFDM transmission in multipath fading channels. We have first designed a correlation function having an impluse-like form, and then, have developed a decision metric based on the standard deviation of the correlation values to estimate the timing offset. From numerical results, it is confirmed that the proposed scheme provides a better MSE and detection performance compared with the conventional schemes in various multipath fading environments. Our future work is to verify the applicability of the proposed scheme to more realistic channel environments.

Acknowledgment

This research was supported by Basic Science Research Program through the National Research Foundation (NRF) of Korea under Grant 2018R1D1A1B07042083 with funding from the Ministry of Education.

References

[1] M. Morelli, C.-C. J. Kuo, and M.-O. Pun, "Synchronization techniques for orthogonal frequency division multiple access (OFDMA): a tutorial review," *Proc. IEEE*, vol. 95, no. 7, pp. 1394-1427, July 2007.

[2] R. V. Nee and R. Prasad, OFDM for Wireless Multimedia Communications, Boston, MA: Artech House, 2000.

[3] T. M. Schmidl and D. C. Cox, "Robust frequency and timing synchronization for OFDM," *IEEE Transactions on Communications*, vol. 45, no. 12, pp. 1613-1621, Dec. 1997.

[4] H. Minn, M. Zeng, and V. K. Bhargava, "On timing offset estimation for OFDM systems," *IEEE Communications Letters*, vol. 4, no. 7, pp. 242-244, July 2000.

[5] K. Shi and E. Serpedin, "Coarse frame and carrier synchronization of OFDM systems: a new metric and comparison," *IEEE Transactions on Wireless Communications*, vol. 3, no. 4, pp. 1271-1284, July 2004.

[6] J. W. Choi, Q. Zhao, and H. L. Lou, "Joint ML estimation of frame timing and carrier frequency offset for OFDM systems employing time-domain repeated preamble," *IEEE Transactions on Wireless Communications*, vol. 9, no. 1, pp. 311-317, 2010.

[7] J. Liu, C. Wei, X. Zeng, J. Lu, and M. Wang, "Research on timing synchronization algorithms for CO-OFDM systems,' in Proc. International Conference on Optical Communications and Networks (ICOCN), 2016.

[8] A. Awoseyila, C. Kasparis, and B. G. Evans, "Improved preamble-aided timing estimation for OFDM systems," *IEEE Communications Letters*, vol. 12, no. 11, pp. 825-827, Nov. 2008.

[9] S. Suyoto, A. Kurniawan, and S. Sugihartono "Timing estimation based on normalized 3rd-order central moment for symmetric correlator in OFDM systems," in Proc. International Conference on Information Technology Systems and Innovation (ICITSI), pp. 135-158, 2014.

[10] S. Suyoto, I. Iskandar, S. Sugihartono, and A. Kurniawan, "Improved Timing Estimation Using Iterative Normalization Technique for OFDM Systems," *International Journal of Electrical and Computer Engineering (IJECE)*, vol. 7, no. 2, pp 905-911, 2017.

Efficient Video-Based Packet Multicast Method for Multimedia Control in Cloud Data Center Networks

Nader F. Mir, Abhishek T. Rao, and Rohit Garg
Department of Electrical Engineering
San Jose State University, California
San Jose, CA, 95195, U.S.A
email: nader.mir@sjsu.edu

Abstract— **The objective of this paper is to demonstrate the best architectural remedy with the required QoS under running that can handle high end real time streaming traffic while multicasting. Since streaming media accounts for a large portion of the traffic in networks, and its delivery requires continuous service, it is required to analyze the traffic sources and investigate the network performance. IP multicasting technology adds tremendous amount of challenge to a network as streamed media delivered to users must be multiplied in volume. In this paper, we first demonstrate a study of the complexity and feasibility of multicast multimedia networks by using different multicast protocols and video sources. In our proposed method, we then create peer-to-peer (P2P) and data center topologies in order to analyze the performance metrics. The implementation and evaluation of the presented methodology are carried out using OPNET Modeler simulator and the various built-in models. Further, we implement performance tests to compare the efficiency of the presented topologies at various levels.**

Keywords-video streaming; cloud data centers; multicast; multimedia; performance evaluation; video codecs.

I. INTRODUCTION

Over the years, major development in the industry have been involved in the integration of various multimedia applications. Delivery of streaming media (video on demand), e-learning with minimum delay and highest quality has been one of the major challenges in the networking industry. Video service providers, such as Netflix, Hulu are constantly changing the architecture in order to service these needs. These service providers face stiff competition and pressure to deliver the next generation of streaming media to the subscribers. The next generation media can be divided into categories: real-time and non-real time. Examples of real time can be live streaming and video conferencing and non-real time can be e-learning and video on demand [1]. The next generation of streaming media [2] involves a large number of subscribers whose delivery is closer aligned with the latest protocols than with the traditional systems. In such cases, it is required that the service providers upgrade their infrastructure and support them [3].

One of the main challenges in the multimedia industry that motivates us to look into it in this paper is multicasting the video streams. IP Multicast is one of the major techniques that can be used for efficient delivery of streaming multimedia traffic to a large number of subscribers simultaneously. Group membership, unicast and multicast routing protocols are mainly required for multicast communications [4]. *Inter Group Membership Protocol* (IGMP) utilized in our study maintains one of the most commonly used multicast protocols at user facility site. IGMP is used to obtain the multicast information in a network. Unicast routing protocols can be distance vector or link state, the latter being preferred due to the dynamic reaction of these protocols to changes in topology. Multicast routing protocols can be integrated with the unicast routing protocol or can be independent of them. Protocols, such as the *Multicast Open Shortest Path First* (MOSPF), depend on the underlying unicast protocols used, whereas protocols, such as *Protocol Independent Multicast* (PIM), are independent on the type of unicast routing protocols used. A combination of IGMP, MOSPF and PIM in sparse mode or dense mode can be used for successful implementation and efficient delivery of multimedia traffic in networks [4].

Multicast routing enables transmission of data to multiple sources simultaneously. The underlying algorithm involves finding a tree of links connecting to all the routers that contain hosts belonging to a particular multicast group. Multicast packets are then transmitted along the tree path from source to destination (single receiver or group of receivers belonging to a multicast group). In order to achieve the multicast routing tree, several approaches have been adopted. Group-shared tree, source based tree and core based tree are some which are explained here.

a. Group-based tree: In this approach a single routing tree is constructed for all the members in the multicast group
b. Source-based tree: This involves constructing a separate routing tree for each separate member in the multicast group. If multicast routing is carried out using source-based approach, then N separate routing trees are built for each of the N hosts in the group [7].
c. Core-based tree: This is a multicast routing protocol, which builds the routing table using a group-shared tree approach. The tree is built between edge and core routers in a network, which helps in transmitting the multicast packets.

MOSPF and PIM use one of the above mentioned approaches in the transmission of packets. As PIM is the multicast routing protocol used in the implementation, we discuss the working of PIM.

PIM is a multicast routing protocol that is independent of the underlying unicast routing protocols used [7]. PIM works in two modes- dense mode and sparse mode. In the former mode the multicast group members are located in a dense manner and the latter approach has the multicast group members distributed widely. PIM uses Reverse path forwarding (RPF) technique in dense modes to route the multicast packets. In dense mode, RPF floods packets to all multicast routers that belong to a multicast group whereas in a sparse mode PIM uses a center based method to construct the multicast routing table. PIM routers which work in sparse mode sends messages to a center router called rendezvous point. The router chosen to be rendezvous point transmits the packets using the group based tree model. As seen in Fig. 1, the RP can move from a group based tree model to a source based approach if multiple sources are specified.

The rest of this paper is organized as follows: Section II provides a detail of our architecture and its functionality and Section III presents a performance analysis of the designed architectures. Finally, Section IV concludes the paper.

II. NETWORK ARCHITECTURE

Network architecture has been designed from service provider's and user's perspective. Network service providers are concerned with the available bandwidth and utilization of resources whereas end user's main concern is with the delivery of streaming media with lowest time and maximum efficiency. In order to obtain the various parameters that are required for the best design of multimedia network, two network models were implemented and analyzed.

A. *Implemented Peer to Peer (P2P) Network Design*

Peer to peer network model is a distributed architecture where the application is transmitted between source and destination through peers. Applications such as music sharing, file sharing use peer-to-peer network model for transmitting the data. A peer-to-peer network was built using the values as shown in Table I. The network architecture shown below represents an organizational division where the admin department is the source of multimedia traffic, which is simultaneously streamed to the remaining departments namely the HR, finance and IT. The topology contains two backbone routers connected back-to-back, a video streaming source is configured and stored in the admin department, where the video frames are encoded with a H.264 codec and generating a frame rate of 15-20 frames per sec. The backbone routers are configured with PIM-DM as the multicast protocol that is responsible to carry multicast packets. The topology diagram can be seen in Fig. 2.

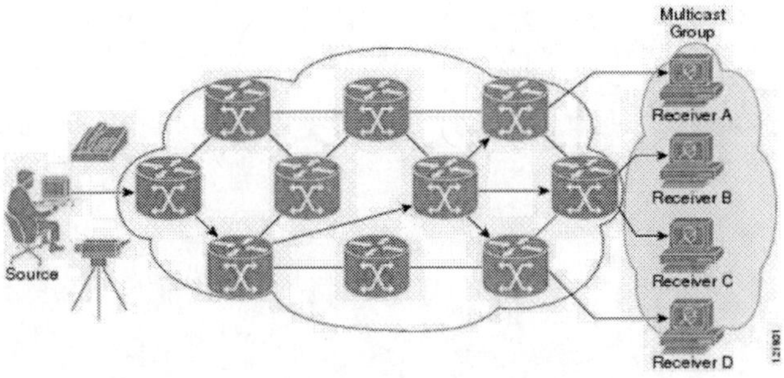

Figure 1. Sample diagram of multicast routing

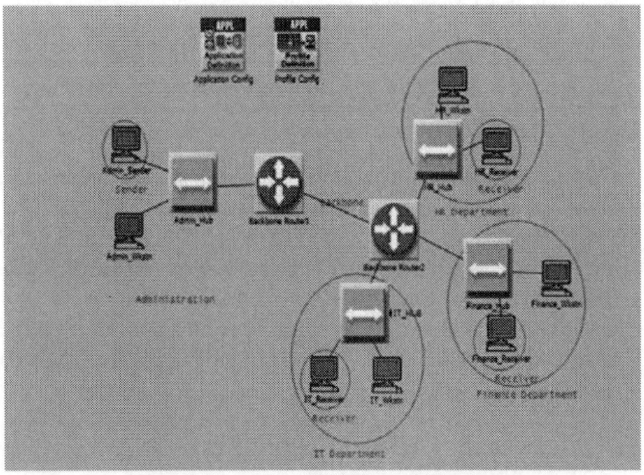

Figure 2. Peer to Peer (P2P) Network Topology

TABLE I. CONFIGURATION PARAMETERS FOR A PEER TO PEER NETWORK DESIGN

Link speed (in Mbps)	Frame size	Frame interarrival rate	Video Codec	Multicast protocol used
100	128x120	10 fps	H.264	PIM-DM
100	128x240	15fps	H.264	PIM-DM
1000	352x240	30 fps	H.264	PIM-DM

B. *Implemented Data center topology*

A data center contains certain facilities for computing, data storage, and other technology resources distributed over different parts of the world. Data center architecture is divided into access, distribution and core layers. Access layers consist of switches that are connected to servers, distribution layer contains switches which transfer the data from access to core layers, and core layer has high speed switching circuitry that transmits the data over WAN links and to other sites. The data center testbed topology implemented in this paper is shown Fig. 3.

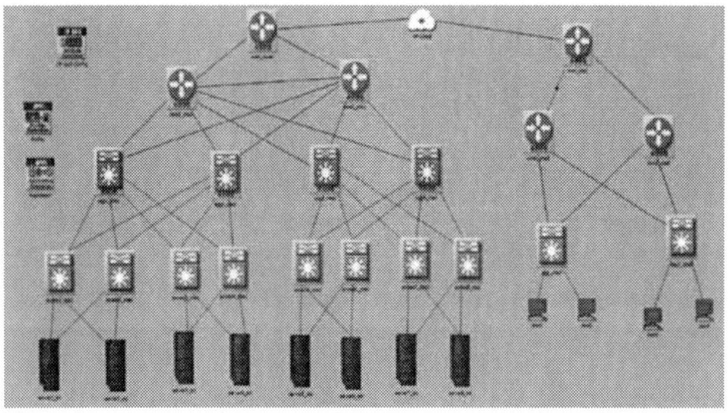

Figure 3. Data Center Topology as the test bed for multimedia streaming

The topology has been implemented taking into account redundancy at all levels. The topology responds dynamically to failures at link, path and device level. Scaling the number of nodes, both horizontally and vertically has been considered in order to analyze the performance metrics of the network. Streaming media content stored at the servers are configured for varying bit rates and varying frame sizes. OPNET simulator has been used as the simulation tool for implementing and testing multicast multimedia traffic detailed metrics that are used for data center implementation has been shown in the Table II.

TABLE II. CONFIGURATION PARAMETERS FOR A DATA CENTER

Number of servers per rack	2
Number of TOR switches used per rack	2
Number of distribution switches per rack	2
Number of core switches per rack	1
Total number of servers	8
Total TOR Switches	8
Total distribution switches	4
Total Core switches	2
Link speeds in data centers	1000 Mbps
Link speeds to WAN	PPP DS3
Video Application and codec used	Video streaming, H.264
Frame sixe	Constant (5000)
Bit rates	Constant (10 fps)

III. PERFORMANCE ANALYSIS

The configuration parameters for used for the performance evaluation are shown below in Table III. Since backbone routers are majorly involved in the transmission of traffic over the internet, Ethernet load across these links has been considered. As the frame size increases load across the backbone links increases, which leads to increase in the delivery of media to destination.

TABLE III. VIDEO CONTENT CONFIGURATION PARAMETERS

Test Name	Frame Size (in bytes)	Video Codec Used	Frame Inter-arrival Time	Ethernet Load Across the Link (packets/sec)
Video1	15,360	H.264	10 Frames/sec	280
Video2	5,000	H.264	Exponential	530

In order to reduce the end to end delay, latency and prioritize traffic Quality of Service (QoS) was implemented. Opnet simulator has various built-in QoS profiles, some of them being WFQ, FIFO, priority queueing. Differentiated services code point based QoS is being used in this implementation wherein based on the priority of traffic delivery, a certain level of service is configured depending on which resources are allocated along the path of delivery.

Now, we present the Ethernet load test – a performance metric which determines the amount of data packets that are carried by the network. Although each link in the network carries data packets WAN / core routers are chosen for analysis. In peer-to-peer topology mentioned earlier, the links connecting the backbone routers are considered, whereas in a data center topology core router links/WAN links have been chosen.

The variation in the graph can be explained as follows. In this case the bit rate and frame size s, both have been kept as exponential increasing functions. From Fig. 4 it can be observed that in a two node network since there is a single link connecting the backbone routers, Ethernet load across these links is considerably higher than that of a multi node model where, PIM builds a tree structure (source based or center based) for sending the multicast packets. As a result, the load is distributed across various links thereby reducing the failure percentage. One more alternative that can be used is port-channel can be configured to distribute the load across the links connecting the routers. Over the time period considered it was observed that the load was higher in a two mode network and lesser in a multi node network.

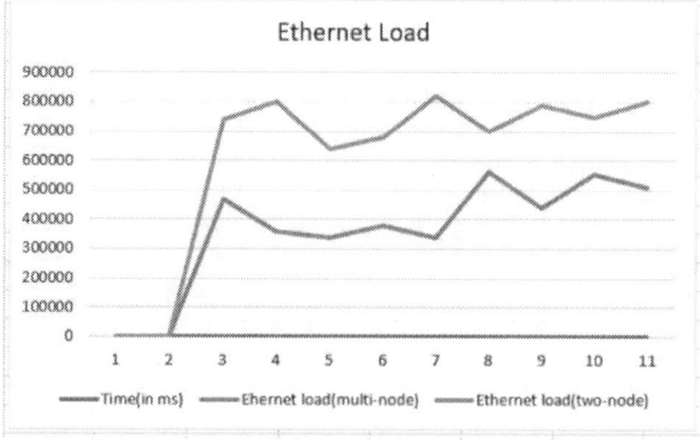

Figure 4. Comparison of Ethernet Load between 2 nodes and multimode case

Our next experiment is concerned with the queueing delay which is the amount of time that a packet waits in the router's queue before being sent onto the network. This is one of the most important parameters for multicast networks as an increase in the queueing delay can cause significant delay in the transmission of packets across the network. Queueing delay can be due to many factors, such as buffer size in a router, router's processing capacity, link speed used, number of hops from source to destination. In this analysis, the queueing delay has been analyzed for a two node and a multi-node environment. From the graphs shown in Fig. 5, it can be observed that although in a two node network links of higher speed were used, when packets of multiple applications arrive, a two node network experienced significant queueing delay which led to the delay in the transmission of packets. Since no QoS was configured all the packets were serviced based on packet arrival times. The graph for a 2 node network shows peaks of highest queueing delay and lows of least queueing delay. This is due to the fact that when packets related to multiple applications arrive there has been peaks of high queue delay and when packets related to single applications arrive less queueing delay has been experienced. In order to have less queueing delay priority traffic can be classified based on QoS policies which helps in serving these packets better.

Next, we consider a test on QoS - a mechanism which is used to analyze the performance of networks. QoS policies configured ensures traffic prioritization and reservation of resources along the path from source to destination. QoS plays a major role in multimedia networks where defining QoS policies defines the traffic priority when real time multimedia traffic and interactive media is involved. Since these types of traffic have rigid delay constraints defining QoS policies for these types can result in prioritizing them when requests for other traffic are in queue.

Simulation results of QoS implementation is shown in Fig. 6. Since real time interactive media could not be created in a simulation environment, two video sources (video1 and video2) were created and video1was configured with a WFQ QoS profile traffic group of video 1 being set to high priority and traffic group of video 2 being set to best effort with no QoS configured. From the plots in the figure, it can be observed that over a period of time when requests arrive for video1 and video2 packets requesting information, video1 is serviced with less packet delay than those packets for video2 while multicast flow is also included in the configuration. Since the IGMP convergence time was 2 min the QoS traffic servicing has started after the first few minutes.

Finally, the latency is our last performance metric to focus on. The latency is the amount of delay involved in transmitting the data from source to destination. For calculating the Latency issues in network different pixel sizes were chosen for analysis. Three different Pixel sizes were configured over a period of time with link speed and other parameters being kept constant. The link speed was defined to be 100 Mbps and pixel sizes of 352x240, 128X240 and 128X120 were defined with frame interarrival rates to be logarithmic. After several tests it was observed that the latency in the transmission of a high quality video was more compared to the latencies of the transmission of a video of lesser resolution as shown in Fig. 7. If a video of high quality has to be transmitted in minimum time, then separate channels can be used for high definition video where source specific trees can be used for routing thereby achieving successful routing of packets.

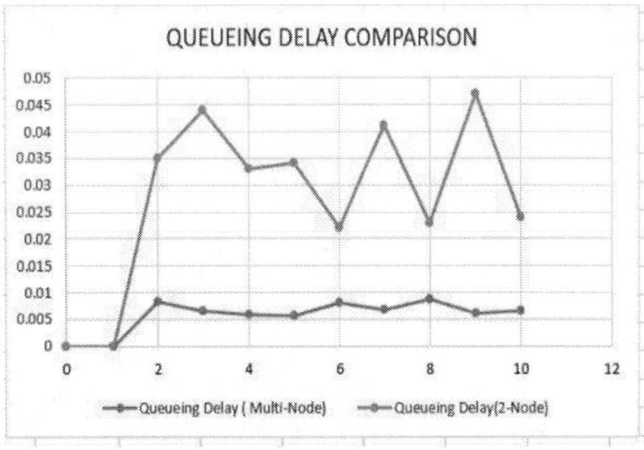

Figure 5. Comparison of queueing delay between 2 nodes and multimode case

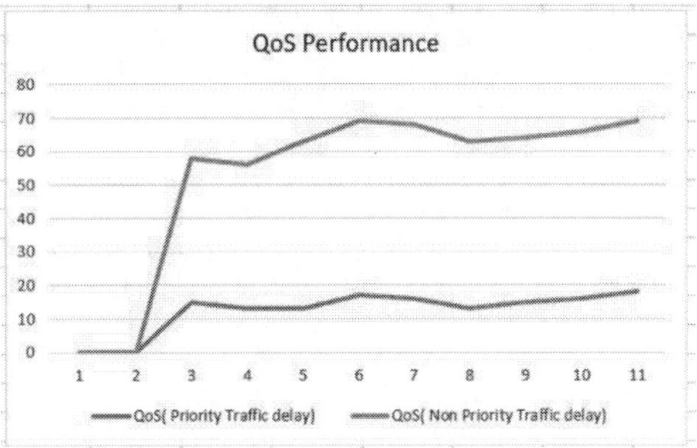

Figure 6. QoS servicing of priority and non-priority traffic

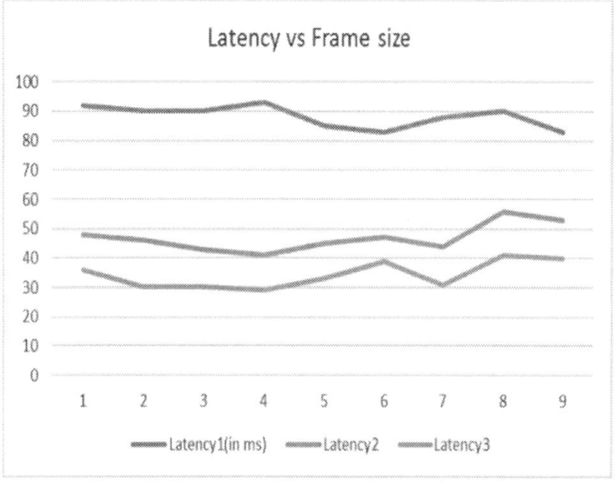

Figure 7. Comparison of Latency of various frame sizes.

IV. CONCLUSION

In this paper, we designed and implemented peer to peer and data center topologies. The two topologies were implemented for various video streaming applications such as video conferencing and video streaming. The parameters of these video sources were changed in to measure the performance metrics of the multicast networks. Parameters such as video codecs, frame size, frame interarrival rate, link speed, QoS were changed for analysis. From the analysis it was observed that a multitier architecture connected to high speed links was best suited for high end real time traffic. Further it was observed that the QoS configuration for these real time traffic reduces the packet end to end delay and the latency of these packets was also less as compared to other packets. Building a multitier not only helped in better load distribution of traffic across links but also this type of topology was better equipped to handle failures at device, links and server levels. This paper also covered the different multicast routing protocols that can be used and how the routing table can be constructed.

REFERENCES

[1] K. Oe, A. Koyama, and L. Batolli, "erformance evaluation of multicast protocols for multimedia traffic," IEEE Xplore document, IEEE 27th International Conference on Advanced Information Networking and Applications (AINA), 2013.

[2] T. Do, K. Hua, and M. Tantaoui, "P2VoD: Providing fault tolerant video-on-demand streaming in peer-to-peer environment." Proc. of the IEEE ICC 2004. Paris: IEEE Communications Society, 2004.

[3] B. Cheng, L. Stein, and J. Hetal, "Grid Cast: Improving peer sharing for P2P VOD," ACM Transactions on Multimedia Computing, Communications, and Applications, vol. 4, 2008.

[4] B. Quinn and K. Almeroth, "IP Multicast Applications: Challenges and Solutions." RFC, 2001, ACM Digital Library.

[5] "OPNET Technologies Inc. OPNET Modeller Product Documentation Release 14.5," OPNET Modeller, 2008.

[6] X. Sun, and J. Lu, "The Research in Streaming Media OnDemand Technology based on IP Multicast," 3rd International Conference on Computer and Electrical Engineering, 2010.

[7] http://www2.ic.uff.br/~michael/kr1999/4-network/4_08-mcast.htm, Access date: July 2018.

[8] Z. Bojkovic, B. Bakmaz, and M. Bakmaz, "Multimedia Traffic in New Generation Networks: Requirements," Journal of Control and Modeling, 2016.

[9] S. Khanvilkar, F. Bashir, D. Schonfeld, and A. Khokhar, "Multimedia Networks and Communication," 2015

[10] X. Wang, C. Yu, and H. Schulzrinne, "IP Multicast Simulation in OPNET," Semantic Scholar, 2015.

Non-binary Encoded STBC-CPM Signals for Wireless Slicing Networks

Piotr Remlein
Chair of Wireless Communications,
Poznan University of Technology
Poznan, Poland
e-mail: piotr.remlein@put.poznan.pl

***Abstract*—The paper considers a wireless transmission system in a multiple-user environment that can support slicing networks. It involves a combination of non-binary convolutional codes and Space Time Block Codes (STBC) technique with narrowband Continuous-Phase Modulation (CPM) for transmission in an uplink channel using the Frequency Division Multiple Access (FDMA) method. Energy efficiency signals, e.g., Continuous Phase Modulation could be used for transmission managing or feedback information signals in return channels of slicing networks. We analyse performance of a transmission in such return channels which apply FDMA method with coded CPM signals via computer simulations. In order to reduce the Bit Error Rate (BER) a concatenation of CPM with non-binary convolutional codes over ring and STBC technique has been used. The spectral efficiency of investigated system is improved by reducing the inter-carrier frequency spacing and using a low-complexity iterative algorithm for Inter-Carrier Interference (ICI) cancellation at the receiver. BER results obtained in computer simulations are presented for the proposed solution. The results suggest that FDMA coded STBC-CPM transmission might constitute a desirable option for return channels in slicing networks.**

Keywords-Continuous Phase Modulation; Frequency Division Multiplexed system; Slicing Networks, Non-binary codes, Inter-Carrier Interference Receiver

I. INTRODUCTION

The network slicing has recently been proposed in the industry solutions for wireless networks as an enabler of network service convergence and on-demand customized services [1]–[3]. The network slicing can support on-demand tailored services for distinct application scenarios at the same time using the same physical network. Supported by network slicing, network resources can be dynamically and efficiently allocated to logical network slices according to the corresponding Quality of Service (QoS) demands. The authors in [4] proposed a network slicing mechanism for network edge nodes to offer low-latency services to users. The mobility management schemes and an optimal gateway selection algorithm to support seamless handover was described. In [5], a resource allocation scheme with the consideration of interference management was presented. In [6], a flexible software defined networking (SDN) based 5G network architecture was proposed. The SDN was used to allocate physical network resources to slices within a local area and to perform scheduling among slices. The research on mobility management in network slicing systems has been focused mostly on SDN based control and handover procedures [6]–[8].

In this article, we propose and investigate the transmission method which can be used in such systems to provide managing and control signals in the return channels.

In the paper, the focus is on FDMA CPM systems which are power and spectral efficiency. We concentrate on the study of non-binary coded STBC-CPM signals in an uplink scenario. The CPM signals are well suitable for wireless return channel transmission through its features constant envelope and its disruptions immunity occurring when signals are transmitted [9]. Additionally, CPM signals are resistant to non-linear distortion of power amplifiers. Multiuser FDMA CPM systems wherein all users employ a portion of the spectrum have been studied in, e.g., [10] – [13].

In order to increase the reliability or bit rate of telecommunication systems, the multi-antenna Multiple Input Multiple Output (MIMO) technique is used more and more often [14]. The technique involves multiple antennas on the transmitter and receiver sides. Employing the MIMO technique in wireless systems allows the use of Space-Time Codes (STC), improving transmission quality [14]. The one of the most popular STC codes and widely used in MIMO systems are space-time block codes (STBC) [15]. These codes are orthogonal and can achieve full transmit diversity specified by the number of transmit antennas. In [16] and [17], the authors studied CPM signals encoded using the so-called orthogonal space-time codes. The CPM signals concatenated with STBC codes are characterized by a low bit error rate attainable at a simultaneously low receiver complexity. Neither of the above solutions for MIMO transmission concerned FDMA CPM systems.

In order to obtain a further improvement in energy efficiency, CPM was combined in classical systems with an external binary Convolutional Encoder (CE) and a mapper. It has been shown that a CPM scheme can be decomposed into a Continuous Phase Encoder (CPE) followed by a memoryless modulator (MM) [18], where the CPE is a CE over a ring of integers [19]. Therefore, a natural way to combine CPM with an outer CE is to use a CE over the same ring of integers. Since the CE and CPE are over the same algebra, no mapper is needed, and an extra coding gain was reported [19].

The literature has discussed the aspects of increasing the spectral efficiency of systems employing CPM and FDMA, e.g., in [12], [13] but STBC coding concatenated with convolutional codes over ring in multiuser scenario has not been taken into consideration.

This paper considers a wireless MIMO FDMA transmission in return channel of slicing networks. It involves a combination of non-binary convolutional codes with STBC and CPM signals for transmission in an uplink channel using the FDMA method. For a more efficient available band utilization, the distances between individual sub-carriers are reduced. Such a solution causes the deterioration of transmission quality due to the occurrence of ICI. In order to reduce the BER in such a system, a combination of CPM with non-binary convolutional codes over a ring has been used and a low-complexity iterative algorithm for ICI cancellation was employed on the receiver side.

The paper is organized as follows. In Section II, properties of CPM modulation are presented. The description of the convolutional codes over ring is included in Section III. Section IV presents the considered system. Section V provides the obtained simulation results. The paper is summarized and concluded in Section VI.

II. CONTINUOUS-PHASE MODULATION

A general form of a continuous-phase modulation describes the following formula [9]:

$$x(t,\alpha) = \sqrt{\frac{2E_S}{T}}\cos(2\pi f_o + \varphi(t,\alpha) + \varphi_0) \quad (1)$$

where E_S is the energy per symbol, T is the symbol interval, f_0 is the carrier frequency, φ_0 is the initial phase, $\boldsymbol{\alpha} = (\ldots, \alpha_{-1}, \alpha_0, \alpha_1, \ldots)$ refers to a sequence of data symbols adopting one of the values from the set:

$$\alpha_i \in \{\pm 1, \pm 3, \ldots, \pm(M-1)\} \quad (2)$$

where M is the cardinality of the set and is typically chosen as a power of 2.

Phase $\varphi(t,\alpha)$, in which the transferred information is included, may be described as follows:

$$\varphi(t,\alpha) = 2\pi h \sum_{i=-\infty}^{\infty} \alpha_i q(t-iT) \quad (3)$$

where h is the modulation index defining the value by which the phase changes in each modulation interval.

CPM signals are characterized by the following parameters: modulation index h, pulse length L and phase response function $q(t)$, or its derivative $g(t)$, the frequency response function. One of the parameters having an influence on the spectral characteristics of CPM signals is the shape of a frequency pulse g(t) [9]. In this paper, CPM signals with a rectangular (REC) pulse are analyzed.

The CPM modulator may be performed as cascade concatenation of a continuous-phase encoder (CPE) and memoryless modulator (MM). Such a system is known as the Rimoldi decomposition [18]. The CPE is a convolutional encoder that performs the function of a CPM modulator memory. The memoryless modulator assigns relevant signal shapes to symbols received from the CPE.

To increase CPM signals' resistance to different types of interference arising during transmission, a connection of the CPM signal modulator system with an external encoder is employed. Most frequently it is a convolutional coder. Such a solution is known as Serially-Concatenated Convolutional Coder (SCCC) [11]. A block diagram of the CE and modulator's serial concatenation is shown in Figure 1.

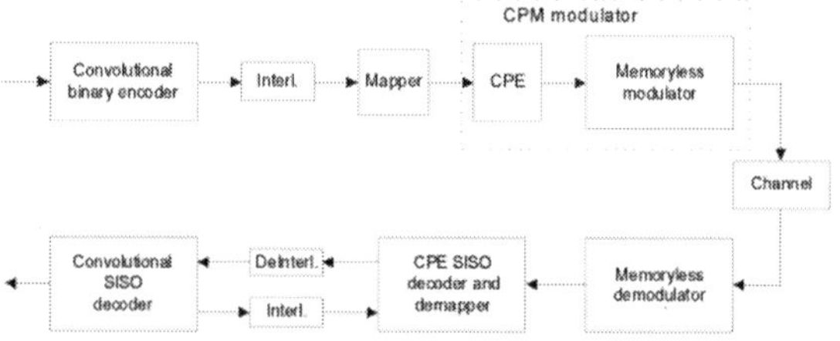

Figure 1. Serially concatenated convolutional encoder CE and CPM modulator.

The convolutional encoder is connected to the modulator by an interleaver and a mapper. The mapper is no needed if external convolutional encoder connected to CPE of CPM modulator are over the same ring of integers modulo-M. The external convolutional encoder CE with rate R_{CE} is equipped with a symbol puncturer with the rate R_{pct}. The overall encoding rate R, with the puncturing operation allowed for, is:

$$R = R_{CE} R_{pct} \quad (4)$$

The discussed method of serially concatenation of the external convolutional encoder and CPM is called in literature a SCCC-CPM and guarantees obtaining of a low BER. There is obtained with the iterative receiver which makes many iterations between the CPE decoder and the decoder of the external convolutional code CE to make a decision on the transmitted information [11].

III. PROPERTIES OF NON-BINARY CONVOLUTIONAL CODES OVER RING

In this paper, we concentrate on the usage of non-binary convolutional codes known as convolutional codes over rings [19]-[21]. These codes in many cases have larger Euclidean distances than binary codes over GF(2) [19] [21].

In Figure 2, it is shown a realization of the systematic feedback convolutional encoder of rate $R_{CE} = k/n$, n=k+1. Input to the encoder, at time t, is information vector U_t with M-ary elements $u_t^{(i)}$ belonging to the ring Z_M={0, 1, 2, ... ,M-1}

$$U_t = (u_t^{(1)}, u_t^{(2)}, \ldots, u_t^{(k)}) \quad (5)$$

The convolutional encoder produces a coded sequence of the symbols which belong to the same ring Z_M

$$V_t = (v_t^{(1)}, v_t^{(2)}, \ldots, v_t^{(n)}) \quad (6)$$

where $n = k+1$.

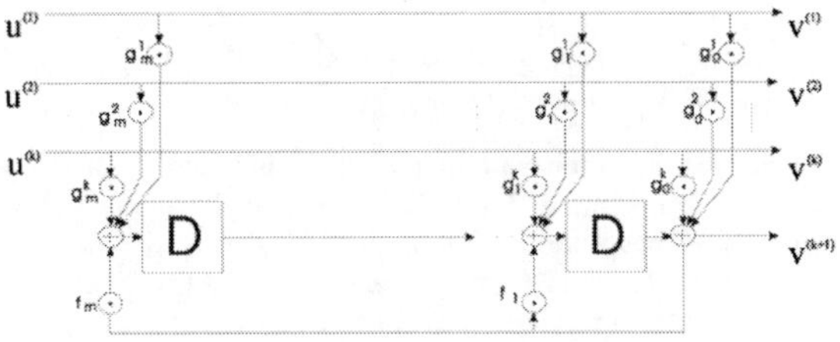

Figure 2. Systematic feedback convolutional encoder over the ring of integers modulo-M (Z_M).

The coefficients of the encoder in Figure 2 are taken from the set {0,...,M-1}. The memory cells are capable of storing the ring elements. Multipliers and adders perform multiplication and addition respectively in the ring of integers modulo-M.

The encoder output V_t at time t due to the input U_t is:

$$V_t = U_t G, \tag{7}$$

where G denotes the generator matrix of the encoder [21].

In Figure 3, we show an example of the systematic convolutional encoder with feedback this is the encoder over the ring Z4 of integers modulo-4.

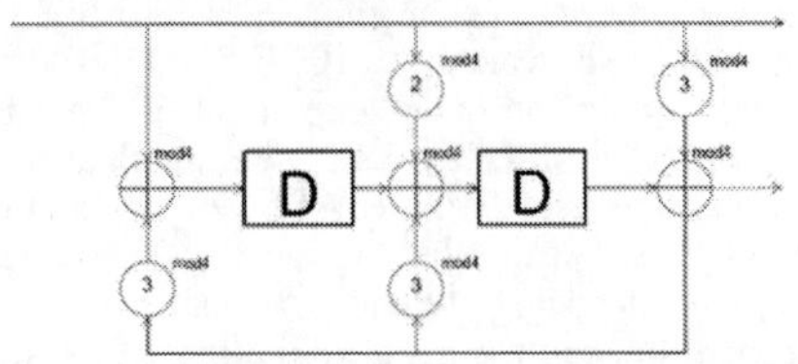

Figure 3. The systematic convolutional encoder over ring $\mathfrak{R}$=Z4.

The code rate is R_{CE}=1/2 (k=1, n=2) and the generator matrix is:

$$G(D) = \begin{bmatrix} 1 & \dfrac{3+2D+D^2}{1+3D+3D^2} \end{bmatrix} \tag{8}$$

At instant t, an information vector with 4-ary symbols belonging to the ring Z_4, inputs the encoder. The convolutional encoder generates encoded vector which contains sequence of the symbols elements belonging to the same ring Z_4. The encoder coefficients in Figure 3 are from the set {0,1,2,3}. The memory cells are capable of storing the ring elements. Multiplications and additions are performed in the ring of integers modulo-4.

IV. FDMA System With Ring Encoded STBC-CPM Signals

In this paper, FDMA system for uplink wireless transmission, using ring encoded CPM signals is analysed. To obtain the best spectral efficiency of the examined system with multiple users, the space between carrier frequencies are minor. The tight inter-carrier frequency spacing between adjacent channels causes strong ICI. To eliminate the ICI in the receiver, an ICI cancelation algorithm is employed. Therefore, it is possible to obtain high spectral efficiency and low bit error rate [13]. Asymptotic spectral efficiency (ASE) can be determined assuming that the signal to noise ratio approaches infinity. ASE is directly proportional to the encoding rate of CE (R_{CE}) and the number of bits falling for one symbol and inversely proportional to the value of normalized spacing between carrier frequencies. ASE for MIMO systems with multiple transmit antennas (M_T) is given by means of the following formula:

$$ASE = \lim_{\frac{E_b}{N_0}\to\infty} SE = M_T \left(\frac{R \ \log_2 M}{\Delta_f T}\right) \tag{9}$$

where E_b/N_0 is the signal to noise ratio, R is the encoding rate, and $\Delta_f T$ is the normalized spacing between inter-carrier frequencies, M-ary modulation. The obtained overall spectral efficiency depends strictly on the number of transmission channels used in the defined frequency band. The encoder rate R is described by relation (4) and can be changed by the rate of the puncturer whose value is changeable in order to obtain specific spectral efficiency.

The CE encoder has a structure determined experimentally, enabling low bit error rate. Performing comparing performance of binary encoded CPM and non-binary CPM, FDMA systems requires selecting codes of equal complexity defined by the number of states. While comparing CE one has to also take into consideration that the comparison in only fair when binary and non-binary systems achieving this same ASE are investigated.

The non-binary code that contributes to acquiring the lowest BER was found for the examined FDMA CPM system. Such defined optimal CE over the ring of Z_4 that has been found in the study and is described by the generator matrix: $[1, D+3, 3D+1]$.

I this paper, we consider the reception of non-binary encodes CPM signals in an FDMA system employing the MIMO technique and STBC coding. An STBC-CPM system analyzed in this paper is based on scheme described in [15].

The transmitted CPM signal vector can be expressed as it was shown in [15].

$$x_t = \left[x_t^1, x_t^2, \dots, x_t^{n_T}\right]^T \tag{10}$$

where n_T is the number of transmit antennas, and T denotes the transpose of the vector [ ].

The modified Alamouti scheme [15] is used for two and four transmit antennas FDMA CPM system. The transmission matrix for two antennas is showed below formula:

$$S = \begin{bmatrix} s_1 & -s_2^* \\ s_2 & s_1^* \end{bmatrix} \tag{11}$$

In this case, the signals transmitted by the first and second antennas into two time intervals are described by equations $x^1 = [s_1 \ -s_2^*]$ and $x^2 = [s_2 \ s_1^*]$, respectively.

Similarly, we can identify the signals in the case of four transmit antennas when transmission matrix is in the form:

$$S = \begin{bmatrix} s_1 & s_2 & s_3 & s_4 \\ -s_2^* & s_1^* & -s_4^* & s_3^* \\ s_3 & s_4 & s_1 & s_2 \\ -s_4^* & s_3^* & -s_2^* & s_1^* \end{bmatrix} \qquad (12)$$

Figure 4 shows a block diagram of the proposed system with STBC coding. At the input, each kth user binary information sequence $\alpha_0, \dots, \alpha_{k-1}$, is Convolutional Encoded (CE), interleaved (Int.) and converted into several (M_T) parallel streams in an STBC encoder. Each data stream is conveyed to one of CPM modulators. In order to achieve higher rates, the CE output is punctured as in [22]: a rate-matching algorithm is used to obtain an appropriate coding rate *R*. The interleaver (Int.) is a symbol, spread (S-random) interleaver [22].

Each user's transmitter consists of an CE, interleaver, STBC encoder and a CPM modulator. The efficiency of an STBC encoder depends on the number of transmit antennas. The STBC encoder considered in the paper uses two or four transmit antennas. Each user signal is characterized by a distinct phase φ_k and delay τ_k, as typically occurs in uplink systems.

The channel model used in the simulation takes into account multipath propagation. The channel model has been implemented as a Taped Delay Line (TDL) and it models a channel with flat fading and Additive White Gaussian Noise (AWGN) [14].

Each receive antenna receives a faded superposition of M_T simultaneously transmitted signals corrupted by additive white Gaussian noise. The fading is assumed to be flat and distributed according to a Rayleigh *pdf*. The random path gains between transmit antenna *m* and receive antenna *p*, $h_{m,p}(t)$ are independent complex Gaussian random variables with zero mean and variance per dimension 1/2. The fading is slow, such that the $M_T x M_R$ fading coefficients are constant during a frame, but vary from frame to frame. The AWGN noise components $n_p(t)$ are independent zero-mean complex Gaussian random processes with power spectral density N_0.

At the receiving end, the system consists of a MIMO MMSE/STBC detector/decoder and a low-complexity iterative algorithm to ICI cancellation [13].

With the assumption of uniform parameters of CPM, and an equal number of transmit antennas M_T for each system user, the signal at the input of the *p*-th receiver antenna is described by:

$$r_p(t) = \sum_{k=0}^{K-1} \sum_{m=0}^{M_T-1} \sum_{n=0}^{B-1} g_{k,m,n}\left(t - n\tau_k, \alpha_{k,m}\right) \cdot e^{j(2\pi k \Delta_f t + \varphi_k)} + n_p(t), \ \ j = 0, \dots, M_R - 1 \qquad (13)$$

where *B* is the number of intervals for which the STBC-CPM signal is transmitted, for the analyzed in the paper system with STBC encoding *B*=2 or 4.

The MMSE/STBC block realizes the STBC decoding and computes the cost function, i.e., minimizes:

$$G_{MMSE} = \sqrt{\frac{n_T}{E_s}} \left(H^H H + \frac{n_T N_0}{E_s} I_{n_T}\right)^{-1} H^H \qquad (14)$$

where *H* is the matrix of channel impulse response estimates, *I* – identity matrix, N_0 – spectral density of noise power, upper index of quantity H^H denotes the Hermitian transpose of matrix *H* and it is the sum of the operations of transpose and complex conjugate of the matrix. Signal *y* from MMSE/STC reaches the ICI cancellation block. The receiver carries out ICI cancellation through a set of single-user MAP detector/remodulator blocks, as described by Perotti et al. [13]. The remodulators make use of the output of the MAP detector to compute the remodulated signal $s_k^{(i)}(t)$ relative to the *k*th user and *i*th iteration. The channel decoder performs two iterations loops. The inner loop is formed by the ICI canceller, the MAP detector, the CPE SISO decoder and the remodulator, while the outer loop involves the CPE SISO decoder, the CE SISO decoder, the interleaver and the deinterleaver between the inner CPE decoder and the outer CE decoder. ICI cancellation can be performed while executing the decoding iterations to enhance the receiver performance. In such a case, after the inner CPE decoder is executed, remodulation is performed. Then, interference cancellation is performed and the CPM receiver, including the inner CPE decoder, is again executed. The decoder starts decoding a received code word executing N_I inner iterations. Then, it executes N_O times an outer iteration followed by an inner iteration. This way, ICI cancellation is performed as part of the decoding iterations and it results in an improved ICI cancellation [13]. On the final outer iteration, a decision is made on the transmitted data symbols $\hat{\alpha}_0, \dots, \hat{\alpha}_{k-1}$.

V. SIMULATION RESULTS

The Monte-Carlo simulation method was used to determine the BER for the described FDMA system with STBC-CPM modulation concatenated with binary CE or CE over the ring. The simulations have been performed with the

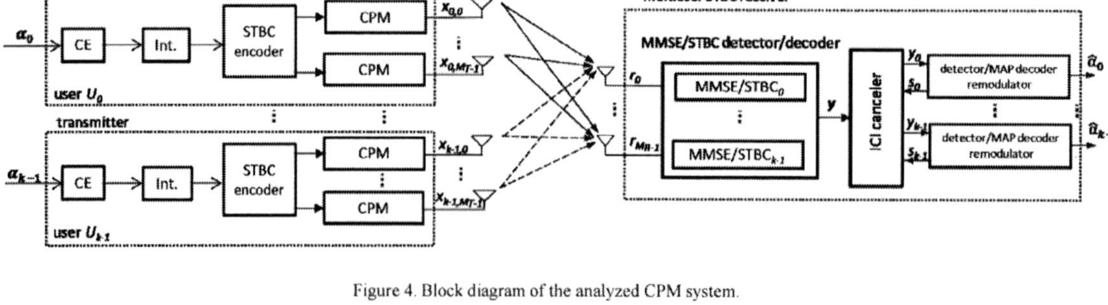

Figure 4. Block diagram of the analyzed CPM system.

aid of a simulation program written in C++ using IT++ libraries, ver. 4.2 [23]. The analysis assumed that each user transmits CPM signals with the same modulation and coding parameters, and of equal strength. We established the ideal power control, this means that the received signal power is the same for all users. It was assumed that the standardized value of the interval between the carrier frequencies of consecutive channels $\Delta_f T$ in the system is equal to 3/4, and that the transmission is performed via 4 neighboring channels (FDMA users). The signals are transmitted through AWGN channel with spectral power density $N_0/2$. The transmitted packets were 1000 bits long. The simulation was stopped if at least 100 errors occurred.

The analysis, for the FDMA system with CPM signals and CE over the ring Z_4, has been performed with reference to binary encoded CPM modulation with the parameters h=1/4, L=1 and the REC shape frequency pulse. The number of iterations in the receiver was experimentally fixed as a good trade-off between receiver performance and complexity.

Two iterations (N_I=2) in the interference cancellation loop have been made and five iterations (N_O=5) in soft output non-binary MAP decoder. The CPM modulator is concatenated with CE over the ring $[1, D + 3, 3D + 1]$ or the binary [7, 5] encoder (from [19], described in octal notation), both with four states. The obtained BER results for the CPM-FDMA systems with CE over a ring were compared with BER for CPM-FDMA systems employing binary CE, which has the same spectral efficiencies.

Figure 5 presents BER for systems employing convolutional encoded CPM modulation concatenated with STBC encoding for different numbers of receive antennas. In this case, each of the four users transmitted signals via one, two or four transmit antennas, and the receiver used one, two or four receive antennas. In this scenario, the error rate at the BER level of 10^{-5} obtained for the 2x2 system was worse than the one obtained for the 4x4 system by about 3 dB and better at the BER level of 10^{-5}than the one obtained for the 1x1 system by about 4dB.

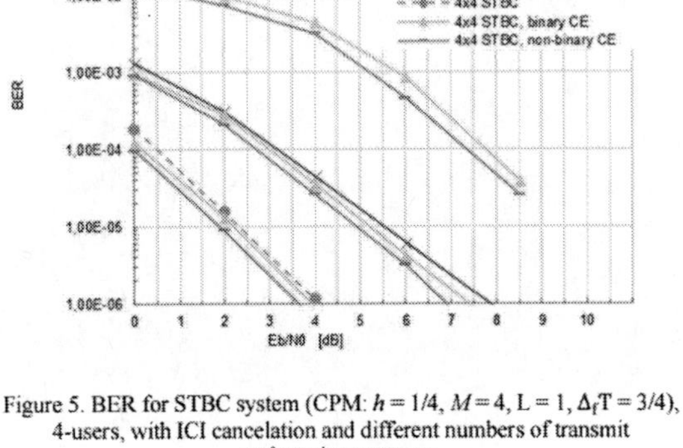

Figure 5. BER for STBC system (CPM: $h = 1/4$, $M = 4$, L = 1, Δ_fT = 3/4), 4-users, with ICI cancelation and different numbers of transmit and receive antennas.

In all cases, we observe that a slight improvement in BER is achieved for the systems using binary encoded STBC CPM signals comparing to the systems without convolutional encoding. We can see that the best results of BER can be obtained when concatenation STBC and non-binary CE was used. It should be noted that, the SE for all the systems 1x1 was equal 1 b/s/Hz, for systems 2x2 amounted 2 b/s/Hz and for 4x4 the SE was 4 b/s/Hz. BER results obtained in computer simulations shoved that proposed solution with non-binary CE gives noticeable improvements compared with results for FDMA systems without convolutional encoding.

VI. Conclusions

In this paper, a multiuser FDMA STBC-CPM transmission with non-binary encoding has been proposed. Through MMSE-based multiuser detection and low-complexity iterative ICI cancellation, considerable improvements in both BER are achieved with respect to single antenna systems, while the multiuser receiver complexity is kept low. A performance evaluation has been presented to demonstrate the superiority of the proposed multiuser FDMA STBC-CPM MIMO system. The study shows that it is possible to increase transmission efficiency by using CPM modulation and concatenation non-binary convolutional encoding with STBC coding for MU transmissions. The presented results show that proposed method can be used in the slicing networks to the transmission of the managing and the control signals.

Acknowledgment

This work has been partially funded by the Polish Ministry of Science and Higher Education within the status activity task 08/81/DSPB/8134 in the year 2018.

References

[1] P. Rost et al., "Mobile network architecture evolution toward 5G," IEEE Commun. Mag., vol. 54, no. 5, pp. 84–91, May 2016.

[2] M. Jiang, M. Condoluci, and T. Mahmoodi, "Network slicing management & prioritization in 5G mobile systems," European Wireless 2016; 22th European Wireless Conference, Oulu, Finland, pp. 1-6, 2016.

[3] Ericsson, Ericsson White Paper: 5G system, Jan. 2015.

[4] J. Heinonen, P. Korja, T. Partti, H. Flinck, and P. Poyhonen, "Mobility management enhancements for 5G low latency services," 2016 IEEE International Conference on Communications Workshops, Kuala Lumpur, pp. 68–73, 2016.

[5] H. Zhang et al., "Resource allocation in spectrum-sharing OFDMA femtocells with heterogeneous services," IEEE Trans. Commun., vol. 62, no. 7, pp. 2366–2377, July 2014.

[6] V. Yazici, U. C. Kozat, and M. O. Sunay, "A new control plane for 5G network architecture with a case study on unified handoff, mobility, and routing management," IEEE Commun. Mag.., vol. 52, no. 11, pp. 76–85, Nov. 2014.

[7] H. Song, X. Fang, and L. Yan, "Handover scheme for 5G C/U plane split heterogeneous network in high-speed railway,"

IEEE Trans. Veh. Technol. vol. 63, no. 9, pp. 4633–4646, Nov. 2014.

[8] S. Kuklinski, Y. Li, and K. T. Dinh, "Handover management in SDN-based mobile networks," 2014 IEEE Globecom Workshops, Austin, TX, pp. 194–200, 2014.

[9] J.B. Anderson, T. Aulin, and C.-E. Sundberg, Digital Phase Modulation. New York, London: Plenum Press, 1986.

[10] D. Bokolamulla and T. Aulin, "Multiuser detection for continuous phase modulation over Rayleigh fading channels," IEEE Communications Letters, vol. 9, pp. 906-908, October 2005.

[11] P. Moqvist and T. Aulin, "Multiuser serially concatenated continuous phase modulation," International Symposium on Turbo Codes, (Brest, France), pp. 211-214, 2003.

[12] A. Barbieri, D. Fertonani, and G. Colavolpe, "Spectrally-efficient continuous phase modulations," IEEE Transactions on Wireless Communications, vol. 8, pp. 1564-1572, March 2009.

[13] A. Perotti, S. Benedetto, and P. Remlein, "Spectrally efficient multiuser CPM Systems," IEEE International Conference on Communications (ICC 2010), Cape Town, South Africa, pp. 1-5, 2010.

[14] E. Biglieri, MIMO wireless communications. Cambridge University Press, 2007.

[15] S. M. Alamouti, "A simple transmitter diversity scheme for wireless communications," IEEE J. Select. Areas Commun., vol. 16, no. 8, pp. 1451–1458, October 1998.

[16] B. Özgül, M. Koca, and H. Deliç, "Orthogonal Space-Time Block Coding for Continuous Phase Modulation with Frequency-Domain Equalization," IEEE Trans. Commun., vol. 57, no. 12, pp. 3579–3584, Dec. 2009.

[17] G. Wang and X.-G. Xia, "Orthogonal space-time coding for CPM system with fast decoding," Int. Symp. Inform. Theory, p. 107, 2002.

[18] B. E. Rimoldi, "A Decomposition Approach to CPM," IEEE Transactions on Information Theory, vol. 34, pp. 260-270, 1988.

[19] M. Xiao and T. Aulin, "Serially Concatenated Continuous Phase Modulation with Convolutional Codes Over Rings," IEEE Trans. Commun., vol. 54, no. 8, pp. 1387-1396, 2006.

[20] J.L. Massey and T. Mittelholzer, "Convolutional codes over rings," 4th Joint Swedish-USSR Int. Workshop Information Theory, pp. 14-18, 1989.

[21] R. A. Carrasco and M. Johnston, Non-binary error control coding for wireless communication and data storage. Wiley, 2009.

[22] D. Divsalar and S. Dolinar, "Weight Distributions for Turbo Codes Using Random and Nonrandom Permutations," JPL TDA Progress Report, vol. 42-122, pp. 56-65, Apr-Jun 1995.

[23] IT++ project, http://itpp.sourceforge.net/4.3.1/, accessed August 2018.

Secure SDN-based In-network Caching Scheme for CCN

Amna Fekih,
Isitcom,
GP1 H-Sousse, Tunisia
emna.fekih@isetso.rnu.tn

Sonia Gaied,
ESST,
Abassi H-Sousse, Tunisia
soniagaied3@gmail.com

Habib Youssef,
CCK,
Univerity campus of Manouba,
Tunisia habib.youssef@fsm.rnu.tn

Abstract—**The different technologies deployment for in-formation exchange on the network and the terminal diver-sity that support them, produce users unwittingly attracted to the Internet that is everywhere in their daily lives. Users require a high Quality of Service (QoS) especially for video streaming applications that generate the main part of the internet traffic. For service providers, it is important to reduce this traffic and increase the Quality of user Experience (QoE). To meet these needs, two additional keys must be exploited: routing and caching. Content Centric Networks (CCN), which is one of the most developed Information Centric Networks (ICN) approaches, offers efficient management of caches at CCN nodes, but the lack of scalable routing is one of the obstacles that slow down its deployment at the internet level. Then, Software Defined Networks (SDN) architecture has been proposed to facilitate programming of the network and to automate the management of the complex architecture but without taking advantage of the capacity of the intermediate caches of the connected nodes. To accomplish tasks, a CCN node uses three tables, Content Store, Forwarding Information Base, and Pending Interest Table, which present attacks to privacy of content requesters and producers. In this paper we propose a Secure In-network Caching Scheme (SICS) for CCN networks based on SDN architecture taking advantage of its global vision. SICS does not only improve cache hit rate and reduce response time, but it also allows to monitor access to CCN routers and detect attacks in order to block them. The results of our model implemented in NS-3 simulator will be presented and evaluated.**

Keywords- CCN; SDN; in-network caching; popularity; Security.

I. INTRODUCTION

The Internet architecture has long been based on the concept of a stack of independent protocols, which requires that all data exchanges via this network must be carried out by establishing communication channels between the network equipment. They are end-to-end, host-centric communications. Today, the Internet is no longer a small network connecting a small community of researchers but it is a large global network connecting virtually all people and organizations around the world. Its use itself is changed too. The evolution of software technologies, improved storage media capabilities, the heterogeneity of terminals and connected equipment, and the nature of frequently used applications such as video streaming [1]. All these factors push researchers to revise, modify and even radically change the current architecture in order to meet the needs of users and service providers without offering temporary solutions to attach them to the Internet architecture.

In recent decades, a simple analysis of network traffic allows us to see that streaming video applications either live or on demand are increasing explosively with the increase in the number of users connected to the Internet. These applications are very greedy in terms of spatial and temporal resources. CCN [2]-[4] is an innovative paradigm that attracts the atten-tion of several researchers. Its principle is to provide content to users instead of establishing communication channels as-sociated with its requests. It aligns with the trend of Internet usage. Users do not look for where and how the requested content will be delivered but they check and compare when at what quality will be received. CCN architecture saves energy consumption and achieves green communication as it dramatically reduces distances by pushing content to users. The important issue in CCN is how to store and manage data packets in local caches of CCN nodes in order to optimize network performance and improve the quality perceived by users. Therefore, this problem is discussed in this article to minimize total network traffic. CCN that is based in-network caching using caches operated at the nodes (Content Store) is able to respond adequately to users' expectations. But the deployment of CCN equipment in existing networks is a critical issue as their design strategies are totally different. In this context, the SDN [5][6] architecture presents a real opportunity, via network programming, to introduce the CCN functionality such as caching and to improve it. The rest of this paper is structured as follows: Related work will be detailed in Section II. The next section describes original CCN and SDN architectures. Section IV provides an overview of our model and details its specifications. The results of our model will be presented and evaluated in Section V. Finally, this work will be closed by a brief conclusion introducing our future work in Section VI.

II. RELATED WORK

In the last years, several works are focused on in-network caching. Although all are aimed at the same objectives, the techniques used are different. [9] exploited the cooperation of the neighbor. The principle was to select cluster headers. Then, they perform cooperative mechanisms of redundancy and elimination avoidance to optimize caching performance. In [10], the authors proposed an admission policy based on a content discovery protocol that allows the router to decide whether the transported content should be cached or not. WAVE [11] is also a system that integrates router collaboration to suggest caching of content blocks to the downstream CCN router. The latter makes caching decision by examining the content polarity and inter-chunk distance. [12] proposed an SDN-based forwarding strategy in CCN as an alternative to the basic strategy that causes additional network traffic due to the flooding of interest packets. For this purpose, the authors used two types of routers, intermediate and gateway routers. The latter are responsible for interconnecting clusters and redirecting inter-cluster interest packets thus minimizing the traffic on the network. [13] split the network into autonomous systems (AS). Each AS selects a control node based on betweenness centrality and cache replacement rate. Their idea is to map SDN features in a CCN network to improve cache performance by exploiting a cache table managed by control nodes.

In CCN, no data packet will be transported on the network if it did not have an explicit request initiated by an Interest packet. These explicit requests slow down DoS attacks [14]-

Although CCN relies heavily on cryptography to authenticate content, the dynamic nature of CCN routers produces vulnerabilities related to these interior tables. The Pending Interest Table (PIT) is critical since it exploits a stateful routing of CCN network. PIT attack [17] is both easy to perform and difficult to detect. A hacker can flood the PIT table with requests for any content that results in the denial of service of pending communications. In contrast to the limited IPv4 / IPv6 address space, the CCN space is delimited opening the door to FIB attacks by generating and publishing content belonging to non-routable domains on CCN network. An adversary looking to decrease caching system performance uses a content store attack DoS. Fortunately, this attack is difficult to achieve since it is greedy in bandwidth.

Our approach is a hybrid solution inspired by the works already mentioned. It is characterized by: i)The control is provided by local SDN controllers whereas CCN routers are simple forwarding devices. ii)A distributed content popularity base that is filled and operated by local SDN controllers. iii)A secure policy-based forwarding strategy defined in [12] where the FIB tables are managed only by the local SDN controllers. iv)A collaboration between CCN routers and their local SDN controller defined in [13] is adopted to ensure the visibility of content stored for CCN routers in the same cluster. v)A new popularity-based caching strategy that associates each content with local popularity according to interest packets processed by transited CCN router. Content may be marked by global popularity. vi)Caching is supplemented by replication and replacement policies based on content popularity, number of CCN router claims (probe packet), and number of hops to retrieve the data.

III. BACKGROUND

In this section, we describe the CCN and SDN architectures. Table 1 presents the different aspects that motivate our work [7][8].

TABLE I. TRADITIONAL IP NETWORKS VS CCN - SDN

	Traditional IP Networks	**Content Centric Networks**	**Software Defined Networks**
Control	Tightly coupled control and data planes	Forwarding strategy is separate from the routing strategy	Decoupling network control and forwarding functions
Native cache	Not supported	Supported (key to success)	Not supported
Routing	Hybrid	Distributed between CCN routers based on prefixes	Centralized, managed by the SDN controllers

A. *CCN Architecture*

Content Centric Networks is the most popular ICN architecture that motivates many researchers with its in-network caching feature.

Naming: In CCN, names are hierarchical. This architecture uses name prefix aggregation to ensure routing scalability. Each content publisher uses a unique prefix to name each content before publishing it. CCN defines two types of packets. Clients use interest packets (INTEREST) to express their requests by specifying the name and the data packet (DATA) is the response provided by any cache router with a copy of the requested content or by the data source.

Routing and Transport: In CCN, each router contains three tables. Each is characterized by one or more well-defined functionalities. The Content Store (CS) is used to cache Named Data Object (NDO). The Pending Interest Table (PIT) that contains a list of pending interests ensures data delivery and the Forwarding Information Base (FIB), which ensures requests forwarding. Subscribers send INTEREST packets to express their requests by specifying the requested NDO that arrive as DATA packets. The data is sent only in response to an interest.

Caching: Unlike other ICN architectures that enable or disable caching, CCN natively supports on-path caching. The Content Store (CS) is a fundamental component in CCN that can be compared to the buffer in IP routers but with a persistent data storage capacity. When an Interest packet is received, each content router verifies its CS first to deliver the requested content directly from its local CS. And when it receives a DATA packet, it stores the transported data in its CS according to the defined caching policy. If there is no match in CS, content router uses the FIB table to forward the request and the PIT table to keep all received interest packets requesting the same NDO. This removes unnecessary transfers on the network.

Security: CCN uses a human-readable hierarchical namespace to improve routing scalability. Security is provided by the content publisher by signing each DATA packet with its secret key. This packet contains a signature over the name, the information included in the message and information about the key used to produce the signature. So the naming in CCN does not contain the publisher key which makes self-certification impossible. The trust in the signing key must be established by external means.

B. SDN Architecture

The technological revolution has made available a diversity of services and a range of equipment and devices that exceed the capacity of the current Internet. This is obvious since the internet was not designed to support these technologies. SDN is a new emerging network paradigm that presents the results of research into virtualization and automation solutions for hardware and software resource management. Open Networking Foundation describes SDN architecture that consists of three layers and different types of APIs allowing communication between them.

Layers and Open API: From the bottom up, the infrastructure layer that consists of network devices that are simple forwarding devices. The control layer is the heart of the SDN architecture. It includes SDN controllers. The latter exploit Open-API to control and manage the forwarding behavior on the network. They communicate via interfaces: southbound, northbound and east/westbound interfaces. The last, application layer where we find user applications such as network virtualization, monitoring and network application.

Features of SDN:

Data/Control planes are decoupled: The decoupling of two planes facilitates the fast automated management and reconfiguration of forwarding devices according to the state of the network.

Logical centralized control: Via its interfaces, the SDN controller can collect information and build a global view of the network.

Network programmability: It is the key feature of the SDN architecture. It ensures scalability and encourages innovation.

Dynamic updating of forwarding rules: This feature aligns with the objectives of managing network resources. enhancing configuration and improving performance thanks to the global knowledge on the network.

OpenFlow Protocol: is the most popular protocol for communication between the infrastructure/control layers. It standardizes information exchange between controller and forwarding devices. Each forwarding device or OpenFlow switch communicates with a controller via secure channel. Each contains one or more flow tables themselves consist of flow entries. These determine how packets will be processed and transmitted.

IV. SECURE SDN-BASED IN-NETWORK CACHING SCHEME

In this section, we describe our secure caching scheme and detail its different features.

A. Overall Architecture

We propose a Secure In-network Caching Scheme for CCN networks based on SDN architecture (SICS) in order to reduce response time, minimize network traffic and improve user perception. SICS is depicted in Figure 1. CCN routers and gateways are located in the data plane with a simple role of forwarding without any control. The control layer consists of SDN controllers.

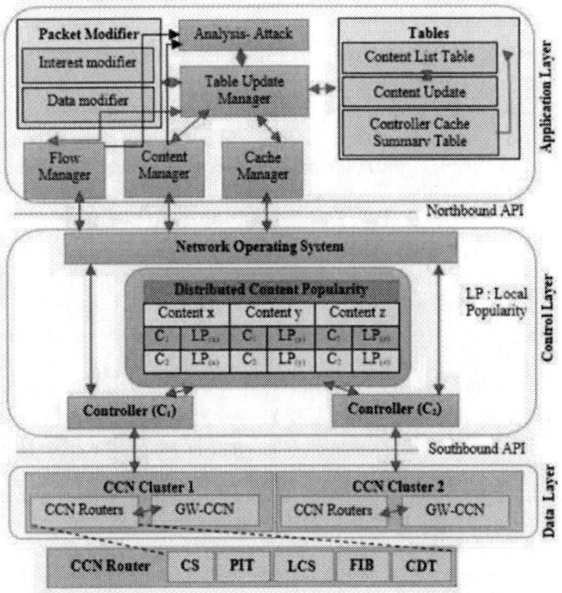

Figure 1. Secure SDN-based In-network Caching Scheme

Interest Packet					
Original CCN Interest Packet	RID	CID	RCID	NHop	P

Data Packet	
Original CCN Data Packet	RCID

Figure 2. Interest and Data packets

Each local controller SDN forms a network global view on its controlled area and manages it by communicating with the forwarding devices by OpenFlow protocol. Automated management and dynamic reconfiguration of network resources are assigned to managers and programmable modules that are specified in the application layer. The module analysis-attack Detection allows the controller to supervise the contents circulating on the network and to block attacks if detected. Flow manager and Update Manager Table are responsible for the flows and routes forwarding of interest packet (respectively data packet) from original producer or any CCN cache to requester. Content Manager manages the transferred content. On the other hand, Cache

Manager and Update Manager Table are responsible for managing and updating the list of contents cached on CCN routers. These are the managers who update Content List Table, Content Update Table, and Controller Cache Summary Table accordingly when they detect network changes.

B. Proposed Packet Types

Our system organizes the packet types into two categories. The first presents the forwarding packets exchanged between clients, CCN routers and SDN controllers. The second includes management packets exchanged between CCN routers and SDN controllers to retrieve, manage, and update CCN caches.

1. *Interest Packet*: Upon receiving client request, the CCN router looks for the content name specified in the packet interest in CS and then in Local Cache Summary Table. In case of cache hit, the response will be transferred to the client. Otherwise, CCN router sends this interest packet to its local controller (as packet_IN in original OpenFlow protocol). To guarantee the transfer of the request from local area to another in case of cache miss, the original CCN interest packet is extended by five fields (Figure 2) to globally identify a request on the network.

2. *Data Packet*: To deliver a requested content, two cases will be possible. the content exists in the same controlled area or another. Then, we adopt the proposal of [12] to add a new field, RCID, to the original CCN data packet to specify the controller ID that initiated the request since the local areas are interconnected by gateways. The RID field (Figure 2) specifies the identifier of CCN router that received the request. The local controller of the area where this CCN router belongs will be recorded in the CID field. The RCID field contains the identifier of the controller where the first CCN router belongs, which will begin the retrieval of requested content. In addition, we add another field, NHop, which presents the number of routers crossed during the delivery of data packet in order to require caching or not. NHop is initialized to 0. While the data packet is transferred to a router belonging to the same controller, NHop will be incremented by 1. If it is forwarded to a router belonging to another controller, NHop will be incremented by 1+ SUM (CCN routers in local controller). The last P field specifying the perimeter of content search. P is local if it is a request to retrieve content from content store of a router belonging to the same local controller. Otherwise, P is extended.

3. *Report Packet*: To inform their local controller of the state of the local caches, the attached CCN routers send periodically the state of their CSs. However, when the CS is changed, the CCN router reports the CS update directly to its controller. CCN router also uses this packet to claim that the CS is full so that the local controller executes the proper content replacement strategy.

4. *Update Packet*: Collecting CS summaries allows the local controller to form a complete view of cached content in con-trolled area, calculate popularity, and replicate when needed. Each local controller advertises its CCST table by sending update packet periodically to its CCN routers. Otherwise, local controller sends an update packet to a specified CCN router requesting replication or delete of a particular content based on its popularity, number of probe packets and the number of hops to deliver it.

Content Store			
Content name	Created_date	Last_update	Data

Forwarding Information Base				
Content name	RID	CID	Requesting router	Requesting controller

Pending Interest Table			
Content name	Created_date	ports	nports

Cache Decision Table			
Content name	RID	CID	CS-MGT

Controller Cache Summary Table / Local CST				
Content name	RID	CID	Priority	Face

Figure 3. CCN router Tables

```
Algorithm 1 : Caching process
Input:  Interest Packet IP, Requested Router RR, Content C
        local popularity LP, threshold
Output: Caching decision
receive Interest packet
compute local popularity of this content in Requested Router LP(C)R
update the local popularity of this content at Controller level LP(C)C
if (LP(C)C > MAX (LP(C)Ci) then
mark interest packet with global popularity
endif
if (interest packet has global popularity) then
Rselected ← betweeness Centrality cache (local controller)
CS-MGT(Rselected) ← 1        -- Rselected : Selected Router
endif
if (LP(C)(RR) == threshold) then
  if (C in CCST) then
    if (priority == G) then    -- Global popularity
    CS-MGT(RR) ← 0
    else
    CS-MGT(RR) ← 1
    CS-MGT(CR) ← 0        --cache router avoid cache redundancy
    endif
  else
    CS-MGT(RR) ← 1
  endif
endif
```

Figure 4. Caching process

5. *Probe Packet*: If CCN router sends a packet interest to local controller, a new entry is added to its PIT table specifying the requested content name and its creation date. Then, a timeout is executed. Once it reaches the value 0 and the router does not receive a data packet. The later sends a probe packet to controller to signal response delay.

6. *Attack_Avoidance Packet*: when SDN controller detects an attack during the content flow analysis, it blocks the source of this attack and forward results to all its CCN routers by an attack_avoidance packet to mark this source.

C. CCN Router Structure

The basic CCN router includes three types of tables: Content Store, Pending Interest table, and Forwarding

Information Base. Content Store (CS) where the content chunks are stored to minimize latency. Pending Interest table (PIT) stores pend-ing requests grouped by name content to reduce network traffic and avoid gateway-level congestion. Forwarding Information Base (FIB) is the forwarding table that plays the same role as FIB in IP protocol. When receiving an interest packet, CCN router first checks its CS. If the content name exists, it provides this content directly to the requester. Otherwise, it checks in PIT. If it exists, it adds an entry specifying the port and deletes this interest packet. If there is no corresponding entry in PIT, then it creates a new entry in PIT and FIB table to transfer to other routers. To achieve our goal, we enrich CCN router with two tables to manage the content store properly and reduce the latency of users. These tables are issued by the local controller. The FIB table is also entrusted to SDN controllers. Upon receiving a data packet, the CCN router checks the CS_MGT field. If it is set to 1 in Cache Decision Table (CDT), this content is saved in CS. Otherwise, the CCN router checks the PIT table and sends the content to the ports that requested. Our system assumes that the network is divided into clusters where each is administered by a local controller. Only the local controller that collects the caching information by the exploit of report packets received from CCN routers when CS is updated. For that we propose Local Cache Summary Table (LCST) in order to publish the CS information between CCN routers present in the same cluster. Local controller groups this information into Controller Cache Summary Table (CCST). In other words, having like a caching cooperation managed by local controller to improve use of cache resources in the same cluster. Interest and data packets structures are presented in Figure 2. Whereas, Figure 3 details tables format in CCN router already described.

D. *Forwarding Process*

The packet forwarding process in SICS is summarized by the activity diagram in Figure 5. A user requests desired content by sending an interest packet to its home CCN router. When this packet is received, our CCN router works in the same way as a basic CCN node for CS and PIT tables. If there is no corresponding entry in PIT, it creates a new entry in PIT. Thereafter, it verifies LCST. If there is an entry for the re-quested content. Then, the P field of the packet interest is set to 0 (default value for external perimeter initialized to 1). Finally, the router checks if there is a FIB entry then it transfers interest packet. Otherwise, it transfers the request to its local controller. The latter exploits two forwarding mechanisms according to the location of data packet. When a request is transferred to the local controller. It first checks P field. Two cases are possible. If P equal 0, then the forwarding mechanism is limited in the cluster managed by local controller. After that, the local controller looks in its CCST table for the corresponding entry. If it exists, it modifies the interest packet and calculates the requested content popularity. Interest packet will forward to a router belonging to the same controller, the number of hops (NHop) will be incremented by 1. Finally, install the rules in FIB and CDT of CCN router while the RID router that stores the requested content is not found. If P is not 0, the forwarding mechanism is beyond the scope of the local controller. Local controller checks CLT to retrieve the default values and then modify the interest packet to retrieve the data packet stored elsewhere. Interest packet will forward to a router belonging to another controller, NHop will be incremented by 1+ SUM (CCN routers in local controller). Finally, it installs the rules in FIB and CDT tables. When receiving a data packet, CCN router checks if there is a match in its PIT table. If it exists, it delivers the packet to the client. Otherwise, data packet is forwarded to its local controller to process it. The latter specifies the requesting router and injects the corresponding route into FIB table.

E. *Caching Process*

In SICS, a CCN Router stores content in its CS if and only if its local controller has validated caching by setting the CS-MGT field to 1 in the CDT table. Whenever the local controller receives a packet interest, it calculates and updates the local popularity of requested content. For effective use of CCN caches, it then compares this probability with the local popularities of this interest packet in other controllers through distributed content popularity base. If local popularity is greater than the maximum of local popularities in other clusters, then local SDN controller marks this interest packet with a global popularity. Our caching strategy is detailed in Figure 4. Two cases are possible. If interest packet is marked with global popularity, then local SDN controller executes betweenness centrality cache to select the best location (selected router) and validates caching by setting the CS-MGT field to 1 in the CDT table of the selected router. If interest packet reaches the local popularity threshold, then local controller verifies its existence in CCST table. If it is present and the associated priority is set to G (Global), then it sets the CS-MGT field to 0. Otherwise, local controller validates caching by setting the CS-MGT field to 1 for requesting router and asks cache router to remove this content and avoid cache redundancy.

F. *Replication Process*

Our caching strategy helps to store the most popular content and exclude unpopular content. Our replication policy takes into account the stored content and seeks to improve the quality perceived by the users. It allows caching of non-popular content based on the number of probe packets that are sent from CCN router to the local controller to warn it of past latency. Each local SDN controller periodically analyzes the received probe packets. Two cases are possible. The requested content is popular so SDN controller checks its CCST table and calculates the time needed to deliver it according to NHop field. It decides content replication if the timeout exceeds the average wait time in the cluster. The content is not popular so SDN controller calculates the number of probe packets received for this content. If it reaches the critical threshold of satisfaction, it selects the CCN router having the maximum popularity for this content where it decides its caching.

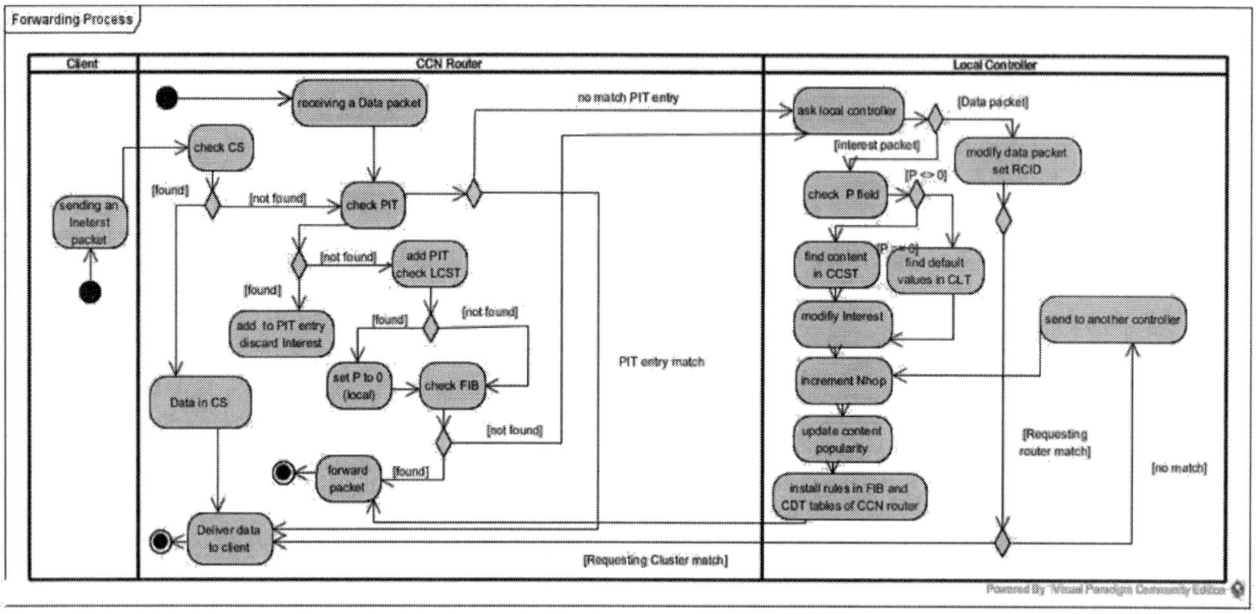

Figure 5. Activity diagram for forwarding process

G. *Replacement Process*

If CS is full, CCN Router sends a Report packet to its local controller that runs the appropriate content replacement policy. First, local controller classifies the contents stored in CS according to their popularities, local or global. Then, they will be put in order. Content with global popularity will be at the top of CS table. While the others will be added at the end of the table. Subsequently, the exclusion will always occur from the end of CS table.

V. SIMULATION AND EVALUATION

In this section, we evaluate the forwarding and caching strategies proposed in CCN based on SDN. We focus on evaluating the efficiency of content delivery, the network traffic rate, the average number of hops during content delivery, and the usage rate of caches. Performance is evaluated using NS3 simulator [21] by integrating OpenFlow and ndnsim modules.

A. *Parameters used for simulation*

The parameters used in the simulation are shown in Table 2. Using the important parameters, we evaluate the average time for content delivery, network traffic, cache hit rate and average hop count compared to original CCN paradigm (BasicCCN), Autonomous System Collaboration Caching Strategy (AS-CCS) [13] and Forwarding Strategy on SDN-based Content Centric Network (FS) [12].

B. *Simulation Results*

With simulation results part, we demonstrate four main comparisons. One is the comparison of the time taken to get data for requests between the proposed forwarding strategy SICS and others. The other is the comparison of total number of interest packets in the network according to different number of requests. Figure 6-a shows the comparison of the time taken for data delivery. It is proved that the proposed forwarding mechanism takes less time for content delivery, which means that it is more efficient than other forwarding strategies such as ASCCS, FS and BasicCCN. In Figure 6-b, as the number of requests gradually increases from 100 to 500 the amount of traffic caused by the packets of interest increases considerably for the BasicCCN strategy since it broadcasts interest packets to all other neighboring routers. On the other hand, ASCCS which exploits the neighbors' cooperation and FS which is characterized by the global vision on the network have almost the same increase for interest packet. But our proposed routing strategy that combines the benefits of other strategies does not have as much impact on the total amount of traffic as BasicCCN does. Figure 6-c shows that SICS can dramatically improve the success rate of the cache, which is shown in the graph clearly compared to the basic CCN architecture and architectures adopted. By increasing the size of the caches the redundancy of the contents will be more possible. Figure 6-d shows that our SICS policy works better than the others by avoiding redundant content in each cluster.

VI. CONCLUSION

In this paper, we proposed a novel Secure In-network Caching Scheme for CCN networks based on SDN architecture (SICS) in order to reduce response time, minimize network traffic and improve user perception. The proposed strategy enables to overcome the problems that the original CCN faces with the help of centralized table management for packet forwarding. Furthermore, simulation result was shown to prove that the efficiency of the average

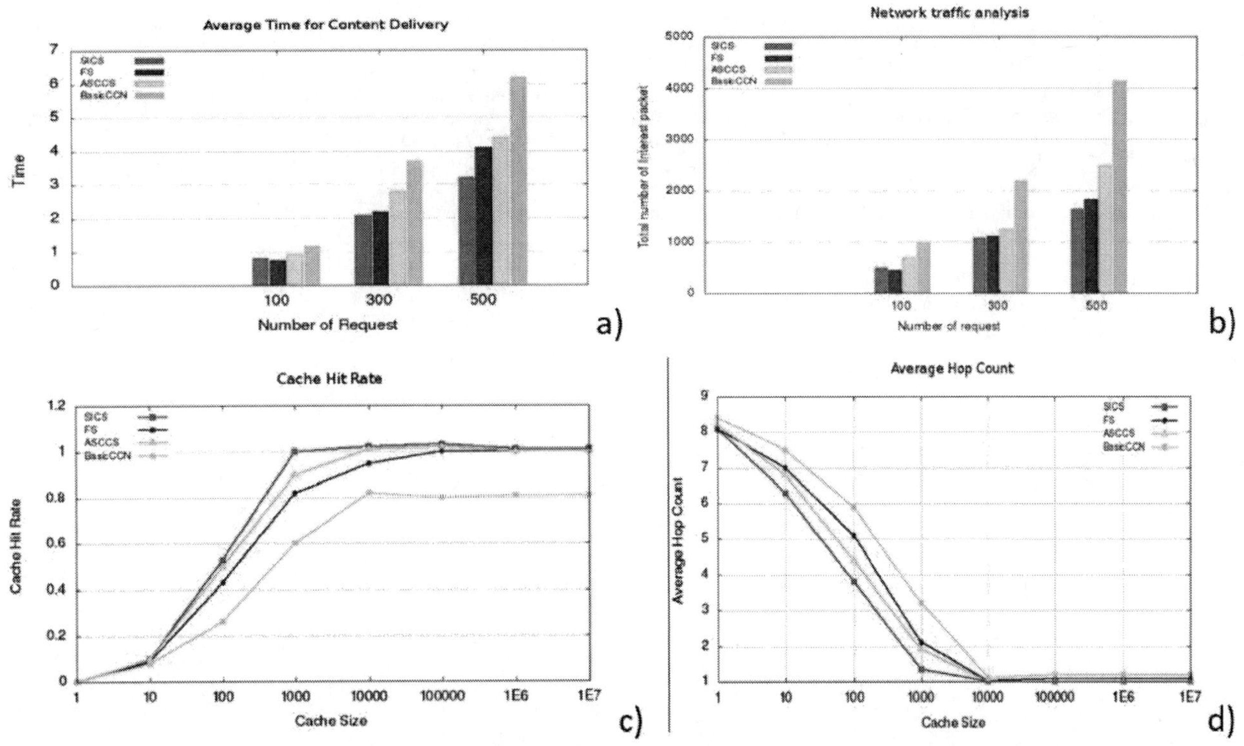

Figure 6. Simulation Results

time for content delivery, network traffic, cache hit rate and average hop count were reasonably decreased. In the near future, these results will be brought together with those of our analytical model presenting our strategy to prove the observed performance improvements. In addition, our current work will be followed by a detailed and deeper study of the compatible protocols between SDN and CCN, guaranteeing the reliability of the proposed architecture.

TABLE II. PARAMETERS USED FOR SIMULATION

Parameters	Symbol	Value
Number of users	U	10
Number of requests	λ	100, 300, 500
File size	F	1
chunk Size	S	10 KB
Forwarding	FS	SICS, ACCCS, FS, and BasicCCN
Cache Size	CS	1, 10, 100, 1000, 10000, 1E5, 1E6, 1E7

REFERENCES

[1] Visual Networking Index: Forecast and Methodology, 2016-2021, CISCO, Tech. Rep., September 2017.

[2] Z. Liu, M. Dong, and B. Gu, "Impact of item popularity and chunk popularity in CCN caching management", In Network Operations and Management Symposium (APNOMS), 18th Asia-Pacific, IEEE, 2016. pp. 1-6, 2016.

[3] C. Yufei, Z. Min , and W. Muqing, "A centralized control caching strategy based on popularity and betweenness centrality in CCN", In Wireless Communication Systems (ISWCS), International Symposium on, IEEE, 2016, pp. 286-291, 2016.

[4] G. Xylomenos, C. Ververidis, and V. Siris, "A survey of information-centric networking research", IEEE Communications Surveys & Tutorials, vol. 16, no 2, pp. 1024-1049, 2014.

[5] A. Lara, A. Kolasani, and B. Ramamurthy, "Network innovation using openflow: A survey", IEEE communications surveys & tutorials, vol. 16, no 1, pp. 493-512, 2014.

[6] F. Bannour, S. Souihi, and A. Mellouk, "Distributed SDN Control: Survey, Taxonomy and Challenges", IEEE Communications Surveys & Tutorials, vol. 20, no 1, pp. 333-354, 2017.

[7] R. Jmal and L.C. Fourati, "Content-Centric Networking Management Based on Software Defined Networks: Survey", IEEE Transactions on Network and Service Management, vol. 14, no 4, pp. 1128-1142, 2017.

[8] A. Fekih, S. Gaied Sonia, and H. Yousef, "A comparative study of content-centric and software defined networks in smart cities", In Smart, Monitored and Controlled Cities (SM2C), International Conference on. IEEE, 2017, pp. 147-151, 2017.

[9] Y. Zhang, H. Qu, and J. Zhao, "A distributed caching based on neighbor cooperation in ccn", In Wireless Communications, Networking and Mobile Computing (WiCOM), 10th International Conference on, Sept 2014, pp. 386–392, 2014.

[10] W. Wong, L. Wang, and J. Kangasharju,"Neighborhood search and admission control in cooperative caching networks", In Global Communications Conference (GLOBECOM), 2012 IEEE, Dec 2012, pp. 2852– 2858, 2012.

[11] K. Cho, M. Lee, and K. park, "Wave: Popularity-based and collaborative in-network caching for content-oriented networks", In Computer Communications Workshops (INFOCOM WKSHPS), 2012 IEEE Conference on. IEEE, pp. 316-3212012.

[12] J. Son, D. Kim, and H.S. Kang, "Forwarding strategy on SDN-based content centric network for efficient content delivery", In Information Networking (ICOIN), 2016 International Conference on, IEEE, pp. 220-225, 2016.

[13] W. Kaili, W. Muqing, and Z. Min, "An autonomous system collaboration caching strategy based on content popularity in CCN", In Personal, Indoor, and Mobile Radio Communications (PIMRC), 2016 IEEE 27th Annual International Symposium on, IEEE, pp. 1-6, 2016.

[14] K. Thakker, C.H. Lung, and P. Morde, "Secure and Optimal Content-centric Networking Caching Design", In Trustworthy Systems and Their Applications (TSA), 2015 Second International Conference on, IEEE, 2015. pp. 36-43.

[15] C. Li, S. Gong, and X. Wang, "Secure and Efficient Content Distribution in Crowdsourced Vehicular Content-Centric Networking", IEEE Access, 2018, vol. 6, pp. 5727-5739.

[16] J. Lv, X. Wang, and M. Huang, "RISC: ICN routing mechanism incorporating SDN and community division", Computer Networks, 2017, vol. 123, pp. 88-103.

[17] D. Goergen, T. Cholez, and J. François, "Security monitoring for content-centric networking", In Data privacy management and autonomous spontaneous security, Springer, Berlin, Heidelberg, 2013. pp. 274-286.

[18] "Software-defined networking: The new norm for networks", Palo Alto, CA, USA, White Paper, Apr. 2012.

[19] O. Blial, M. Ben Mamoun, and R. Benaini, "An overview on SDN architectures with multiple controllers", Journal of Computer Networks and Communications, 2016, vol. 2016.

[20] B.A. Nunes, M. Mendonca, and X.N. Nguyen, "A survey of software-defined networking: Past, present, and future of programmable networks", IEEE Communications Surveys & Tutorials, 2014, vol. 16, no 3, pp. 1617-1634.

[21] https://www.nsnam.org/ [retrieved: November 2017].

Reliability-aware Optimization of the Controller Placement and Selection in SDN Large Area Networks

Eugen Borcoci, Stefan Ghita
University POLITEHNICA of Bucharest - UPB
Bucharest, Romania
Emails: eugen.borcoci@elcom.pub.ro, stalghita@gmail.com

Abstract — **For large networks SDN-controlled, distributed control plane solutions are proposed, to solve the scalability problems generated by the SDN control centralization principle. In a multi-controller environment, the Controller Placement Problem (CPP) should be solved. Additionally, in a dynamic networking context, including possible failures of links or nodes, a forwarder node could try to select an available and reachable controller among those alive. Although several studies have been published, the above problems are still open research issues, given the various network contexts, providers' policies and possible multiple optimization criteria. Multi-criteria decision algorithms can provide valuable solutions. This paper extends a previous work, considering in the developed model some reliability aspects of the distributed SDN control and an extension to a dynamic controller selection method.**

Keywords* — *Software Defined Networking; Multi-criteria optimization; Controller placement; Controller selection; Forwarder nodes assignment; Reliability;

I. INTRODUCTION

Software Defined Networking (SDN) has as basic principles the decoupling of the architectural *Control Plane* (CPl) w.r.t *Data Plane* (DPl) and also CPl centralization in SDN controllers. In the case of large network environments, scalability problems of the CPl appear [1]. The usual solution for this is a distributed multi-controller implementation of the SDN control plane. Different flat or hierarchical organizations for a multi-controller SDN control plane have been developed, e.g., in [2][3].

Note that in a basic approach, the *SDN controller* (SDN-C) is understood as a control entity placed in a geographically distinct location, i.e., a particular physical network node. However, recently, the *Network Function Virtualization* technologies [4] allow that several logical SDN-Cs realized in a virtual manner (notation will be vSDN-C) can be collocated in the same physical node. In the following text we suppose the basic approach; however the models developed in this paper can be as well applied also to a virtualized environment.

Actually, several associated problems exist together with *controller placement problem* (CPP) itself. Some examples are: how the network topology is specified - flat or clustered; what criteria are considered to solve the CPP; number of controllers - predefined or not; failure-free or failure-aware metrics (e.g., considering backup controllers and node/link failures); how the DPl forwarders nodes are assigned to controllers (in static or dynamic way, i.e., depending on actual network conditions and network provider policies), and others. The evaluation of the degree of optimality of different approach can be studied on some simplified topologies – in order to compare the efficiency of approaches or, on real specific network topologies. Several studies [5-15] considered various aspects and solutions of the CPP problem.

In a real network environment, it has been apparent that there is no uniform and strict placement rule to be the best for any SDN-controlled network. Dynamic nodes addition and deletion can happen and, in such cases, a forwarder could dynamically select an appropriate controller, if it has enough pertinent and updated information. This is *called controller selection problem* (CSP) and can be considered as an extension of the CPP [11].

The CPP is a non-polynomial (NP) -hard problem [5]; therefore different pragmatic solutions have been proposed, many of them with specific optimization criteria, targeting performance in failure-free or failure-aware approaches. Examples of specific, individual criteria could be: to maximize the controller-forwarder or inter-controller communication throughput; reduce the latency of the path connecting them; limit the controller load imbalance; find an optimum controllers' placement and forwarder-to-controller allocation, offering a fast recovery after failures (controllers, links, nodes). Also, other specific optimization goals could be added to the above list, depending on specific context (wire-line, wireless/cellular, cloud computing and data center networks) and on some specific business targets of the Service Provider.

One main issue is that different optimization criteria could lead to different solutions; so, a multi-criteria global optimization could be a better approach.

The paper [12] provides a contribution on multi-criteria optimization algorithms for the CPP not by developing specific single-criterion algorithms (many other studies already did that) but to achieve an overall optimization by applying *multi-criteria decision algorithms* (MCDA) [16]. The input of MCDA is the set of candidates (an instance of controller placement is called a candidate solution). Examples have been analyzed, on some real network topologies, proving the usefulness of the approach.

This paper extends the model of [12]*; several reliability aware criteria have been added to the CPP solution. Also the novel CSP extension is introduced, being appropriate for a dynamic network context. It is shown that the same basic MCDA can be applied in both static and dynamic context, but with different sets of criteria. Simulation experiments and novel results are presented.*

The structure of the paper is described here. Section II is a short overview of related work. Section III revisits several metrics and optimization algorithms and presents some of their limitations. Section IV revisits the framework for MCDA-RL (the variant which is called "*reference level*") as a simple but powerful tool to solve the CPP and CSP problems. Section V presents the implementation performed to validate the MCDA proposed model in reliability-aware approach, and outlines the simulation experiments performed. Section VI offers few samples of simulation results to illustrate the validity of the approach. Section VII presents conclusions and future work.

II. RELATED WORK

This short section is included mainly for references. More comprehensive overviews on published work on CPP in SDN-controlled WANs are given in [10-13]. The goal is to find those controller placements that provide high performance (e.g., low delay for controller-forwarder communications) and also create robustness to controllers and/or network failures.

Heller et al. [5] have early shown that it is possible to find optimal solutions for realistic network instances, in failure-free scenarios, by analyzing the entire solution space, with off-line computations (the metric is latency). Going further, the works [6][7][8][9][14] additionally considered the resilience as being important with respect to events like: *controller* failures, *network links/paths/nodes* failures, *controller overload* (load imbalance). The *Inter-Controller Latency* is also important and, generally, it cannot be minimized while simultaneously minimizing controller-forwarders latency; a tradeoff solution could be the answer.

The works [6][8] developed several algorithms for real topologies, considering reliability of SDN control, but still keep acceptable latencies. The controller instances are chosen as to minimize connectivity losses; connections are defined according to the shortest path between controllers and forwarding devices. Muller et.al. [9] eliminate some restrictions of previous studies, like: single paths, processing (in controllers) of the forwarders requests only *on-demand* and some constraints imposed on failover mechanisms. Hock et.al. [7] adopted a multi-criteria approach for some combinations of the metrics (e.g., max. latency and controller load imbalance for failure-free and respectively failure use cases).

In a recent work [11], K.Sood and Y.Siang propose to transform the CPP problem into *Controller Selection Problem* (CSP), i.e., consider the dynamics of the network and make controller selection. They explore the relationship between traffic intensity, resources requirement, and QoS requirements. It is claimed that to optimize the control layer performance, the solutions must be topology-independent and adaptive to the needs of the underlying network behaviour. They propose a topology independent framework to optimize the control layer, aiming to calculate the optimal number of controllers to reduce the workload, and investigate the placement/location of the controllers. However, their first declared objective has been not to determine the optimal placement of controllers in the network, but to motivate the CSP.

In [12], a multi-criteria algorithm is used (applicable for an arbitrary number of decision criteria) to solve the CPP; validation of results have been presented for some real network topologies [17][18].

This paper extends the [12] work, by adding new reliability–aware metrics and also outlines the usage of the multi-criteria method to solve the controller dynamic selection problem (CSP).

III. EXAMPLES OF CONTROLLER PLACEMENT METRICS AND ASSOCIATED ALGORITHMS

This section is a short presentation of a few typical metrics and optimization algorithms for CPP and CSP. A more detailed presentation of them can be found in [12]. Considering a particular metric (criterion) an optimization algorithm can be run for a given metric, as in [5][6][7][9].

However, this paper goal is not to develop a new particular algorithm based on a given single metric, but to search for a global optimization. The individual metrics presented in this section can be embedded in a multi-criteria optimization algorithm.

The SDN-controlled network is abstracted by an undirected graph G(V, E), with V - set of nodes, E – set of edges and $n=|V|$ the total number of nodes. The edges weights represent an additive metric (e.g., *propagation latency* [5]).

A basic metric is *d(v, c): shortest path* distance from a forwarder node $v\in V$ to a controller $c\in V$. We denote by C_i a particular placement of controllers; $C_i \subseteq V$ and $|C_i| < |V|$. The number of controllers is limited to $|C_i|= k$ for any particular placement C_i. The set of all possible placements is denoted by $C = \{C_1, C_2 \ldots\}$. Some metrics are basic, i.e., failure-free; others take into account failure events of links or nodes.

An important metric for SDN control is the *latency* between nodes. Note that, while it has a dynamic nature, in some simplified assumptions it is estimated as a static value.

A. *Failure-free scenarios*

- *Forwarder-to-controller latency*

In Heller's work [5], two (failure-free) metrics are defined for a given placement Ci: *Worst_case_latency* and *Average_latency* between a forwarder and a controller. An optimization algorithm should find a placement C_{opt}, where either *average latency* or *the worst case latency is minimized.*

The work [15] proposes an algorithm to *maximize the number of nodes within a latency bound*, i.e., to find a placement of *k* controllers, such that they cover a maximum number of forwarder nodes, but with an upper latency bound of each forwarder latency to its controller.

- *Inter-controller latency*

The SDN controllers should inter-communicate and therefore the inter-controller latency is important. For a given placement C_i, one can minimize the *maximum latency between two controllers*. Note that this can increase the forwarder-controller distance (latency).Therefore, a trade-off is necessary, thus justifying the necessity to apply some multi-criteria optimization algorithms, e.g., like Pareto frontier - based ones [7].

B. Failure-aware scenarios

In such scenarios controller and/or network failures events are considered. The optimization process aims now to find trade-offs to preserve a convenient behavior of the overall system in failure cases (controllers, or nodes, or links).

- *Multiple-path connectivity metrics*

If multiple paths are available between a forwarder node and a controller [9], this can exploited in order to reduce the occurrence of controller-less events, in cases of failures of nodes/links. The goal in this case is to maximize connectivity between forwarding nodes and controller instances. A special metric can be defined as:

$$M(C_i) = \frac{1}{|V|} \sum_{c \in C_i} \sum_{v \in V} ndp(v,c) \tag{1}$$

The *ndp(v,c)* is the *number of disjoint paths* between a node v and a controller c, for an instance placement C_i. An optimization algorithm should *find the placement* C_{opt} *which maximizes* $M(C_i)$.

- *Controller failures*

To minimize the impact of such failures, the latency-based metric should consider both the distance to the (primary) controller and the distance to other (backup) controllers. For a total number of *k* controllers, the failures can be modeled [7], by constructing a set C of scenarios, including all possible combinations of faulty controller number, from 0 of up to k - 1. The *Worst_case_latency_cf* will be:

$$L_{wc-cf} = \max_{v \in V} \max_{C_i \in C} \min_{c \in C_i} d(v,c) \tag{2}$$

The optimization algorithm should find a placement which *minimizes the expression* (2).

Note that in failure-free case, the optimization algorithm tends to rather equally spread the controllers in the network, among the forwarders. To minimize (2), the controllers tend to be placed in the center of the network, such that in a worst case, a single controller can take over all control. However, the scenario supposed by the expression (2) is very pessimistic; a large network could be split in some regions/areas, each served by a primary controller; then some lists of possible backup controllers can be constructed for each area, as in [9]. The conclusion is that an optimization trade-off should be found, for the failure-free or failure cases. A multi-criteria approach can provide the solution.

- *Nodes/links failures*

For such cases, the objective could be to find a controller placement that minimizes the number of nodes possible to enter into controller-less situations, in various scenarios of link/node failures. A realistic assumption is to limit the number of simultaneous failures at only a few (e.g., two [7]). If more than two arbitrary link/node failures happen simultaneously, then the topology can be totally disconnected and optimization of controller placement would be no longer useful.

For a *placement* C_i of the controllers, an additive integer value metric $Nlf(C_i)$ could be defined, as below: consider a failure scenario denoted by f_k, with $f_k \in F$, where F is the set of all network failure scenarios (suppose that in an instance scenario, at most two link/nodes are down); initialize $Nlf_k(C_i) = 0$; then for each node $v \in V$, add one to $Nlf_k(C_i)$ if the node v has no path to any controller $c \in C_i$ and add zero otherwise; compute the maximum value (i.e., consider the worst failure scenario).

$$Nlf(C_i) = \max Nlf_k(C_i) \tag{3}$$

The optimization algorithm should find a placement *to minimize* (3), where *k should* cover all scenarios of F. It is expected that increasing the number of controllers, will decrease the *Nlf* value. However, the optimum solution based on the metric (3) could be very different from those provided by the algorithms using the latency-based metrics.

- *Load balancing for controllers*

It is desired a good balance of the node-to-controller distribution is desired. A metric $Ib(C_i)$ will measure the degree of imbalance of a given placement C_i as the *difference between the maximum and minimum number of forwarders nodes assigned to a controller*. If the failure scenarios set S is considered, then the worst case should evaluate the maximum imbalance as:

$$Ib(C_i) = \max_{s \in S} \{ \max_{c \in C_i} n_c^s - \min_{c \in C_i} n_c^s \} \tag{4}$$

where n_c^s is the number of forwarder nodes assigned to a controller c. Equation (4) takes into account that in case of failures, the forwarders can be reassigned to other controllers and therefore, the load of those controllers will increase. An optimization algorithm should find that *placement which minimizes the expression (4).*

IV. MULTI-CRITERIA OPTIMIZATION ALGORITHMS

SDN controllers' placement and/or selection may involve several particular metrics (as summarized in Section III). If optimization algorithms for particular metrics are applied, then one can obtain different non-convergent solutions. Actually the CPP and CSP problems have naturally multi-criteria characteristics; therefore MCDA is a good way to achieve a convenient trade-off solution.

This paper uses the same variant of MCDA implementation as in [12], i.e., the *reference level (RL) decision algorithm* [16] as a general way to optimize the controller placement, and controller selection, for an arbitrary number metrics. The MCDA-RL selects the optimal solution based on normalized values of different criteria (metrics).

The MCDA considers *m* objectives functions (whose values, assumed to be positive should be minimized). A solution of the problem is represented as a point in a space R^m of objectives; the decision parameters/variables are: v_i, i = 1, ..m, with $\forall i$, $v_i \geq 0$; so, the image of a candidate solution is $Sl_s=(v_{s1},v_{s2}, ..,v_{sm})$, represented as a point in R^m. The number of candidate solutions is S. Note that the value ranges of decision variables may be bounded by given constrains. The optimization process consists in selecting a solution satisfying a given objective function and conforming a particular metric.

The basic MCDA-RL [16], defines two reference parameters: r_i=*reservation level*=the upper limit, not allowed to be crossed by the actual decision variable v_i of a solution; a_i=*aspiration level*=the lower bound beyond which the decision variables (and therefore, the associate solutions) are seen as similar (i.e., any solution can be seen as "good"- from the point of view of this variable). Applying these for each decision variable v_i, one can define two values named r_i and a_i, i= 1, ..m, by computing among all solutions s = 1, 2, ..S:

$$r_i = \max\ [v_{is}],\ s = 1, 2, ..S \qquad a_i = \min\ [v_{is}],\ s = 1, 2, ..S \qquad (5)$$

An important modification is proposed in [16], aiming to make the algorithm agnostic versus different nature of criteria. The absolute value v_i of any decision variable is *replaced* with *distance from it to the reservation level*: r_i-v_i; (so, increasing v_i will decrease the distance); *normalization* is also introduced, in order *to get non-dimensional values, which can be numerically compared* despite their different nature. For each variable v_{si}, a ratio is computed:

$$v_{si}' = (r_i - v_{si})/(r_i - a_i),\quad \forall s,i \qquad (6)$$

The factor $1/(r_i-a_i)$ - plays also the role of a weight. A variable for which the possible dispersion of values is high (max – min has a high value in formula (6)) will have lower weight and so, greater chances to be considered in determination of the minimum in the next relation (7). On the other side, if the values *min, max* are rather close to each other, then any solution could be enough "good", w.r.t. that respective decision variable.

The basic MCDA-RL algorithm steps are (see also [12]):

Step 0. Compute the matrix $M\{v_{si}'\}$, s=1...S, i=1...m

Step 1. Compute for each candidate solution *s*, the minimum among all its normalized variables v_{si}':

$$\min_s = \min\{v_{si}'\};\ i=1...m \qquad (7)$$

Step 2. Select the best solution:

$$v_{opt} = \max\ \{\ \min_s\ \},\ s=1, ..S \qquad (8)$$

Formula (7) selects for each candidate solution *s*, the worst case, i.e., the closest solution to the reservation level (after searching among all decision variables). Then the formula (8) selects among the solutions, the best one, i.e., that one having the highest value of the normalized parameter. One can also finally select more than one solution (quasi-optimum solutions in a given range). The network provider might want to apply different policies when deciding the controller placement; so, some decision variables could be more important than others. A simple modification of the algorithm can support a variety of provider policies. The new normalized decision variables will be:

$$v_{si}' = w_i(r_i - v_{si})/(r_i - a_i) \qquad (9)$$

where $w_i \in (0,1]$ is a weight (priority), depending on policy considerations. Its value can significantly influence the final selection. A lower value of w_i represents actually a higher priority of that parameter in the selection process.

V. MCDA-BASED IMPLEMENTATION FOR SDN CONTROLLER PLACEMENT

A proof of concept simulation program (written in Python language [12]) has been constructed by the authors, to validate the MCDA–RL based CPP problem and allocation of forwarders to controllers. The program has been extended in this work with reliability evaluation features.

The simplifying assumptions (they could be also seen as limitations) of the model studied here, are: the network architecture is flat, i.e., no disjoint regions are defined; the network graph is undirected; any network node can be a forwarder but also can collocate a controller; when computing paths or distances, the metrics are additive; the number of controllers is predefined; the data traffic aspects and signaling interactions are not considered yet.

A. The MCDA basic model

The basic model to solve the CPP problem considered in this paper has two working modes:

a. static mode - the input data are: network graph (overlay or physical), link costs/capacities, shortest path distances between nodes (e.g., computed with Dijkstra algorithm based on additive metric), desired number of controllers, etc.).

Two phases are defined:

(1)*Phase 1*:

1.1. Define the criteria (i.e., the parameters of interest) and their priorities. The decision variables could be anyone, among those of Section III.

1.2. Compute all controller placements C1, C2, ... (i.e. the set of candidate solutions). The number of placements is C_n^k (n= total number of network nodes; k= number of controllers).

1.3. Compute the *values of the normalized metrics for each possible controller placement (i.e. future MCDA candidate solution)*, by using specialized algorithms and metrics like those defined in Section III.

The Phase 1 phase has as outputs the set of candidate solutions (i.e., placement instances) and values to fill the entries of the matrix M defined in Section IV. The Phase 1 computation could be time consuming (depending on network size) and therefore, could be performed off-line [5]. For instance, in a real network, a master SDN controller having all these information can perform these computations.

(2) *Phase 2*: MCDA-RL: define r_i and a_i, for each decision variable; eliminate those candidates having parameter values out of range defined by r_i; define – if wanted – convenient weights w_i for different decision variables; compute the normalized variables (formula (6)); run the MCDA Step 0, 1 and 2 of the (formulas (7) and (8)).

The Phase 2 provides the CPP solution.

b. dynamic mode – the input information is the total number of network nodes and desired number of controllers. The graph (which could be full-mesh or not) and costs of the links are randomly generated by a simulation program. The desired total number of nodes and the number of controllers should be specified as inputs in the program.

B. Reliability aware model

As shown in Section III, more realistic scenarios consider the possible occurrence of controller and/or network failures events. The optimization process aims now to find trade-offs to preserve a convenient behavior of the overall system in failure cases.

- *Backup controllers*

A simple static solution for assignment of forwarders to primary and backup controllers is presented below. We assume that CPP has been solved for a given network. Therefore the identities of controller nodes are known. The simplest assignment of forwarders to controllers is to consider the shortest paths between a forwarder to a controller. So, an algorithm computes all distances from a forwarder F_i to each controller CT_k and selects the closest CT_m as primary controller (based on shortest path between F_i and any controller) and the next (let it be CT_n in the ordered list of distances) as a backup controller.

However, while the primary controller placement after first run of the MCDA) is a global trade-off optimum, there is no guarantee that in case of node/link failures the placement of the backup controller is optimum, given the individual choice of the secondary/backup controller for each forwarder node.A natural solution is to add a novel criterion to the MCDA set of decision parameters.

An auxiliary algorithm is used to compute a simple metric (mean distance to a backup controller) to be added to MCDA. We introduce a novel decision variable *dist_backup* and perform the following computation (for each possible controller placement Ci containing the controllers CT_1, CT_2, ...CT_k):

```
For each forwarder Fi, i=1..N
 Do
   Dist_backup = 0;
   Compute dist. from Fi to any CTj, j=1..k;
   Dist_backup=Dist_backup + second_shortest_cost;
 Od
   Dist_backup_avg = Dist_backup/N;
```

This `Dist_backup_avg` can be added as a new decision variable to MCDA (maybe with appropriate wight) Therefore, the optimization will select a solution which considers also the backup controller nodes in the factors influencing the selection. Note that the inclusion of the backup controllers will increase the number of computations in the Phase 1.2 from C_n^k to C_n^{2k}.

- *Load balancing for controllers*

As shown in Section III, a good balance of the node-to-controller distribution is desired. If the number of nodes is N and the number of controllers is k, then the average number of nodes allocated to a controller is N/k. A simple new metric can be added to the set of MCDA criteria. This decision variable *D_avg* will measure the deviation of the number of nodes allocated to a controller CT_i, i.e., n_i from the average value N/k, and averaging this for all controllers.

$$D\_avg = (1/N)\ \mathrm{Sum}\ |(n_i - N/k)|,\ i= 1\ldots k \qquad (13)$$

Again, this variable can get an appropriate weight in the optimization process.

- *Nodes and link failures*

Nodes and link failures could appear in the network. Evaluation of effects of such events could be taken into account by adding new decision appropriate parameters in the set of MCDA input multi-criteria. Here, we adopted a different approach. Given that most important metrics are forwarder-controller latency, inter-controller latency, load balancing of the controllers, optimization of the placement of the primary and backup controllers, the MCDA has been first run to produce controllers' placement optimization based on these important parameters. Then the simulation program allows some events to happen (e.g., nodes or link failures). The MCDA has been run again and produce a new placement after removing the entities in failure. Finally the placement produced in the updated conditions can be compared with the initial one, to evaluate if significant changes appeared. In such a way one can evaluate the robustness of the initial placement, and decide if that can be preserved or must be changed.

Two input parameters have been defined in the model:

nf- number of nodes supposed to fail

ef – number of links supposed to fail.

The specific nodes and links which will fail will be selected as to to simulate the "worst case", i.e., those nodes having the lowest cost of the adjacent links and, respectively those links having the least costs. If after second run of the MCDA, the initial placement of the controllers does not change, this means that initial placement has enough good robustness properties. Of course, this result will depend on selection of nf and ef values, for a given N nodes of the graph.

C. Controller placement optimization- Simulation program

The user interface of the simulation program is presented in Figure 1.

```
stefan@mint ~/Desktop/simulator_mcda $ python mcda.py -h
usage: mcda.py [-h] [-a [A]] [-w [W]] [-i [I]] [-b [B]] [-l [L]] [--dynamic] [-n N] [-c C] [-nf NF] [-ef
EF] [--debug]

Multi-criteria optimization algorithm
Optional arguments:
  -h, --help    show this help message and exit
  -a [A]        Average latency - failure free scenario. Expects a weight (priority) in interval (0, 1].
  -w [W]        Worst case latency - failure free scenario. Expects a weight (priority) in interval (0, 1].
  -i [I]        Inter controller latency. Expects a weight (priority) in interval (0, 1].
  -b [B]        Average latency - failure scenario. Expects a weight (priority) in interval (0, 1].
  -l [L]        Controller load-balancing. Expects a weight (priority) in interval (0, 1].
  --dynamic     Generate dynamic undirected graph
  -n N          Number of graph nodes. Valid only in dynamic mode.
  -c C          Number of controllers in graph. Valid only in dynamic mode.
                Allowed values are between N/3 and N/7
  -nf NF        Number of nodes that fail. Valid only in dynamic mode. Allowed  values: 1.. N-C.
  -ef EF        Number of edges that fail. Valid only in dynamic mode. Allowed  values: 1 ..N-C.
  --debug       Prints some computing results for debugging purposes.
```

Figure 1. The interface of the MCDA CPP simulation program

The decision parameters considered have been: *average* and *worst* latency between a forwarder and controller, *inter-controller* latency and *load balancing* related parameter. The program can be run isn static or dynamic mode, with any number and set of criteria among those presented in the interface. Note that if wanted, the set of decision parameter can be enriched; the only needed modification is the number of columns of the matrix M.

Several numerical examples and results of the basic CPP solutions have been already presented in the work [8]. The current version of the implementation added reliability feature presented in Section IV.B.

The pseudo-code of the simulation program for dynamic mode is presented below, in high level view.

```
Start
   Generate the random graph;
   Generate all controlers' placements;
   Run MCDA;
   If link_failures specified then eliminate from
the graph a number of ef links having the minimum
costs;
   If node_failures specified then eliminate from
the graph a number of nf nodes;
   If failures_produced
      Then {generate modified graph; Run MCDA;}
   Display the graphs;
Stop
```

D. Dynamic controller selection

In a dynamic network context, the controller choice (CSP) can be performed in a dynamic way. The multi-criteria algorithm can be as well applied in such cases. We consider here only the situations in which controller/node/link – related occur.

In the static approach the backup controllers are predefined; the placement is selected by the optimization algorithm. For a real network, the algorithm can be run offline in a management center (in a hierarchical organization of the control plane, this could be a master SDN controller). This center is supposed to know all information in order to run MCDA-RL algorithm. The aspects related of providing these information constitute a separate problem, which is not studied in this paper.

Supposing that a forwarder looses its connectivity with its controller, it can act in two ways; a. try to connect to a known backup controller; b. select among several by running a MCDA algorithm. The input information for MCDA (decision criteria) could be : identities/addresses of possible SDN controllers; degree of load for those controllers (this could be periodically communicated to the forwarder by a master SDN controller); local information observed by the forwarder, like connectivity to different nodes/controllers, etc. So, the forwarder can select based on MCDA-RL a novel controller.

VI. Samples of Results

This section will shortly present samples of results, in order to prove the validity of approach. The experiments are reliability feature related.

- *Load balancing for controllers*

Figure 2 shows an example in which the network graph has been dynamically generated with N=6 nodes and k= 2 controllers. The decision criteria have been *inter-controller latency* (weight = 1) and *balancing criterion* (weight = 0.5, i.e. twice higher priority). The MCDA program is run with parameters :

```
stefan@mint$ python mcda.py -i 1 -l 0.5 --
dynamic -n 6 -c 2
```

The results obtained are: controllers in CT_0 and CT_3. The allocation of forwarders are :

```
Controller 0 has allocated node(s): 0, 2, 4.
Controller 3 has allocated node(s): 1, 3, 5.
```

One can see that while the inter-controller latency is not minimum, the allocation of the forwarders to controllers is balanced (3 forwarders per each controller).

- *Links and node failures*

If the unique parameter considered in MCDA would be the average latency of the forwarders to backup controllers, then one would expect that the resulting placement could be enough resilient to a low number of nodes and/or link failures.

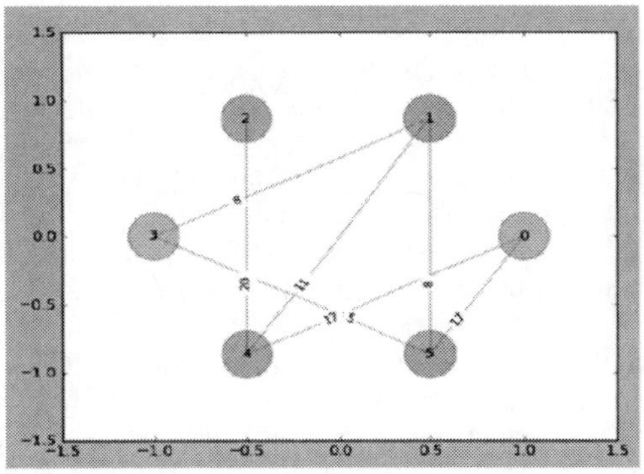

Figure 2. Simple example of a balanced allocation of the forwarders to controllers (after MCDA run)

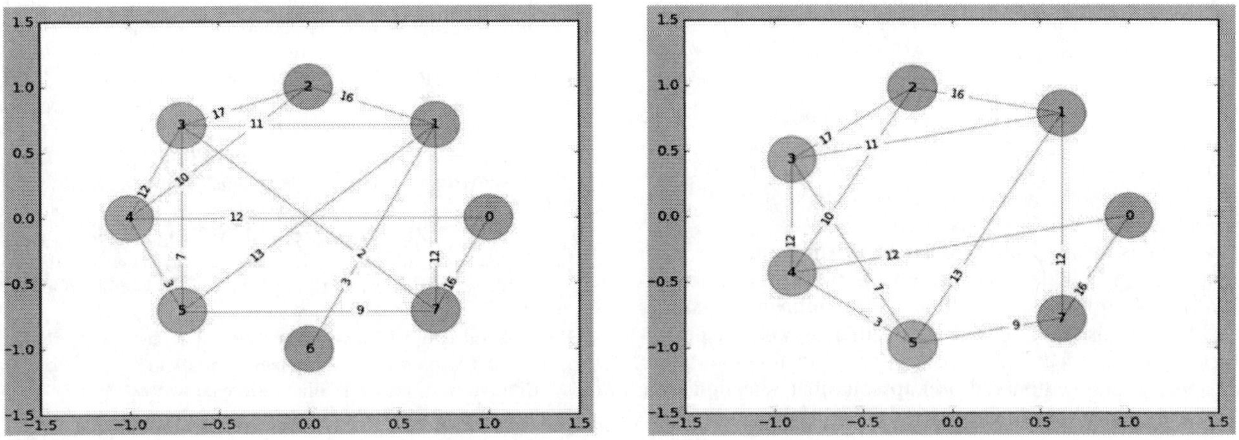

Figure 3. Example of placement resilient to link failures
Left: placement before link failures; Right: placement after some links failures.

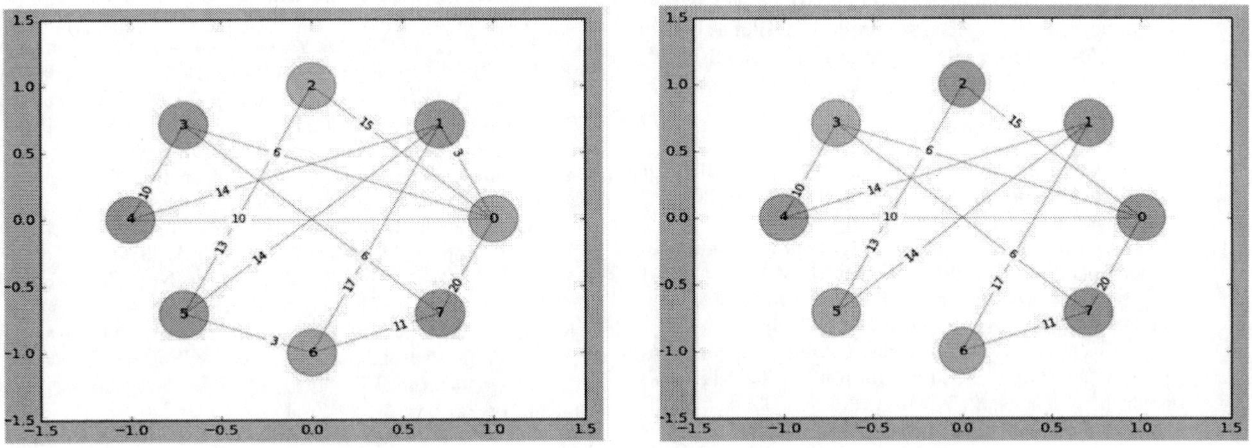

Figure 4. Example of placement non-resilient to link failures
Left: placement before link failures; Right: placement after some links failures.

Figure 3 shows such an example, by presenting the graphs resulted after running the program with the command:

```
python mcda.py -b --dynamic -n 8 -c 3 -ef 2
```

In this example, we have N=8 nodes and c= 3 controllers; the number of failure links ef=2.

One can see that after some links failure (1-6, 3-7) still the controller placement (after running MCDA on the reduced graph) is the same, i.e., 3,4,5.

On the other side, if the initial criterion of MCDA is the to minimize the average latency between the forwarders and controllers (parameter introduced with weight = 1) the optimum placement after some link/nodes failures will be different (Figure 4). The command for such a run is:

```
python mcda.py -a --dynamic -n 8 -c 3 -ef 2
```

These examples illustrate the power of the MCDA algorithm where various sets of criteria and different priorities (driven by policies) can be considered.

VII. Conclusions and Future Work

This paper extended the study [12], on using multi-criteria decision algorithms (MCDA) to optimally place the controllers in large SDN, based networks. The MCDA advantage is that it can produce a tradeoff (optimum) result, while considering several weighted criteria, part of them even being partially contradictory.

In this study, a previous simulation program has been extended to include reliability aware metrics in the multi-criteria optimization algorithm. The optimum controller placement has been found, while different weights policy-driven have been introduced. Also, forwarder-controller mapping optimization and backup controller selection have been also considered. The examples given demonstrate the flexibility of the approach in selecting the best solution while considering various criteria.

Future work will be done to a more deep study of the dynamic possibilities to apply the multi-criteria based selection of the SDN controllers and to consider also aspects of signaling traffic (inter-controller). Hierarchically organized SDN control planes are also open research topics for CPP and CSP problems.

References

[1] S. H. Yeganeh, A. Tootoonchian, and Y. Ganjali, "On Scalability of Software-Defined Networking", IEEE Comm. Magazine, pp. 136-141, February 2013..

[2] A. Tootoonchian, and Y. Ganjali, "Hyperflow: a distributed control plane for openflow" in Proc. INM/WREN, 2010, https://pdfs.semanticscholar.org/f7bd/dc08b9d9e2993b3639 72b89e08e67dd8518b.pdf, [retrieved: 5, 2018].

[3] T. Koponen, , M.Casado, , N.Gude, J.Stribling, L. Poutievski, et.al., "Onix: a distributed control platform for large-scale production networks," in Proc. OSDI, 2010, https://www.usenix.org/legacy/event/osdi10/tech/full_papers /Koponen.pdf, [retrieved: 5, 2018].

[4] B.Han, V. Gopalakrishnan, L. Ji, and S. Lee, "Network Function Virtualisation: Challenges and Opportunities for Innovations". IEEE Communications Magazine, pp. 90-97, February 2015.

[5] B. Heller, R. Sherwood, and N. McKeown, "The controller placement problem," in Proc. HotSDN, pp. 7–12, 2012, https://dl.acm.org/citation.cfm?id=2342444, [retrieved: 5, 2018].

[6] H. Yan-nan, W. Wen-dong, G. Xiang-yang, Q. Xi-rong, and C. Shi-duan, "On the placement of controllers in software-defined networks", ELSEVIER, Science Direct, vol. 19, Suppl.2, pp. 92–97, October 2012, , http://www.sciencedirect.com/science/article/pii/S10058885 1160438X, [retrieved: 1, 2018].

[7] D. Hock, M. Hartmann, S. Gebert, M. Jarschel, T. Zinner, and P. Tran-Gia, "Pareto-Optimal Resilient Controller Placement in SDN-based Core Networks," Proceedings of the ITC, Shanghai, China, 2013, https://ieeexplore.ieee.org/document/6662939/, [retrieved: 1, 2018].

[8] Y. Hu, W. Wendong, X. Gong, X. Que, and C. Shiduan, "Reliability aware controller placement for software-defined networks," in Proc. IM. IEEE, pp. 672–675, 2013, https://ieeexplore.ieee.org/document/6573050/, [retrieved: 1, 2018].

[9] L. Muller, R. Oliveira, M. Luizelli, L. Gaspary, and M. Barcellos, "Survivor: an Enhanced Controller Placement Strategy for Improving SDN Survivability", IEEE Global Comm. Conference (GLOBECOM); 12/2014, https://ieeexplore.ieee.org/document/7037087/, [retrieved: 1, 2018].

[10] G.Wang, Y.Zhao, J.Huang, and W.Wang, "The Controller Placement Problem in Software Defined Networking: A Survey", IEEE Network, pp. 21- 27, September/October 2017.

[11] K. Sood and Y.Xiang, "The controller placement problem or the controller selection problem?", Journal of Communications and Information Networks, Vol.2, No.3, pp.1-9, Sept.2017.

[12] E. Borcoci, T. Ambarus, and M. Vochin, „Multi-criteria based Optimization of Placement for Software Defined Networking Controllers and Forwarding Nodes," The 15th International Conference on Networks, ICN 2016, Lisbon, http://www.iaria.org/conferences2016/ICN16.html, [retrieved: 5, 2018].

[13] S.Yoon, Z.Khalibl, N. Yaakob, and A.Amir, "Controller Placement Algorithms in Software Defined Network - A Review of Trends and Challenges", MATEC Web of Conferences ICEESI 2017 140, 01014 DOI:10.1051/matecconf/201714001014, 2017.

[14] Y. Zhang, N. Beheshti, and M. Tatipamula, "On Resilience of Split-Architecture Networks" in GLOBECOM 2011, http://citeseerx.ist.psu.edu/viewdoc/download?doi=10.1.1.69 1.795&rep=rep1&type=pdf, [retrieved: 5, 2018].

[15] D. Hochba "Approximation algorithms for np-hard problems", ACM SIGACT News, 28(2), pp. 40–52, 1997,.

[16] A. P. Wierzbicki, "The use of reference objectives in multiobjective optimization". Lecture Notes in Economics and Mathematical Systems, vol. 177. Springer-Verlag, pp. 468–486.

[17] Internet2 open science, scholarship and services exchange. http://www.internet2.edu/network/ose/, [retrieved: 4, 2018].

[18] S. Knight, H. X. Nguyen, N. Falkner, R. Bowden, and M. Roughan, "The Internet Topology Zoo," IEEE JSAC, vol. 29, no. 9, 2011, pp.1765-1475..

Green ISP Networks via Hybrid SDN

Krishna P. Kadiyala
Telecommunications Engineering Program
The University of Texas at Dallas
Richardson, Texas 75080
Email: krishna.kadiyala@utdallas.edu

Jorge A. Cobb
Telecommunications Engineering Program
The University of Texas at Dallas
Richardson, Texas 75080
Email: cobb@utdallas.edu

Abstract—**The development of Software Defined Networking (SDN) has introduced many benefits to legacy networks, and has become an appealing option for Internet service providers. However, doing a complete overhaul of an existing service provider network in an attempt to transform it into an SDN network is a significant economical, managerial, and technical challenge. To alleviate this, research is being performed on *hybrid* SDN networks, in which only a few routers are retrofitted to become capable of supporting SDN. In this paper, we study the impact that hybrid SDN can have on the electrical power usage of a service provider network. Most service providers have redundant routers for reliability purposes and for accommodating changes in traffic over time. These redundant routers and links are always powered on, wasting valuable energy. This waste of energy can be mitigated by identifying such routers and shutting them down. However, turning off routers reduces the number of routing paths available to the intra-domain routing protocol, which in turn has the consequence of having an unbalanced traffic load in the egress links of the service provider. This increase in link utilization experienced by some egress links leads to packet losses and long packet delays. To alleviate this, we propose retrofitting a few legacy routers to become SDN routers. By introducing just a few well-placed SDN routers, the routing flexibility increases within the network. This allows for a larger number of routers to be shutdown without exceeding a desired upper bound on link utilization. We present heuristics for choosing which routers should be augmented with SDN capabilities, and we evaluate via simulation their impact on the number of routers than can be powered down.**

Keywords–Software-defined networking; Traffic engineering; Load balancing.

I. Introduction

A current concern in society is minimizing the use of energy. This concern has reached various aspects of computing, and it is often referred to as green computing. In this paper, we focus on reducing the energy usage of enterprise networks, in particular, Internet Service Providers (ISPs).

Traditional ISP networks are over-provisioned to accommodate for unforeseen link/router failures and sudden traffic bursts. These redundant routers and links are always powered on, even though they may not be used to their full capacity at all times. Thus, the energy consumption of the network remains consistently high while the network resources remain under-utilized. By identifying such routers and shutting them down, we are able to reduce the energy consumption of the network to a certain extent.

However, an important consideration when shutting down internal routers of an ISP is that the reduced network must satisfy the traffic demand without over-provisioning the peering (i.e., external) links of the ISP. That is, the links joining the ISP to other Autonomous Systems (AS) must not reach high utilization levels. This is critical due to the fact that the peering links of an AS have been shown to be bottlenecks and are often the cause for congestion [1]. Shutting down routers may lead to high utilization of the peering links of the AS since all the traffic may have to exit through only a few reachable egress routers.

Balancing the traffic over the egress links is dependent upon the routing paradigm of the ISP. The typical routing paradigm consists of moving the transit traffic along the least-cost path. That is, each internal link has a cost, and the traffic arriving via an ingress link exits via the egress link where the total cost of the links traversed is the least. This is commonly known as hot-potato routing (HPR). Although HPR minimizes the cost of transit traffic through the ISP's network, it does not take into consideration the load on the peering links of the ISP, which, as mentioned above, are the most likely to become congested.

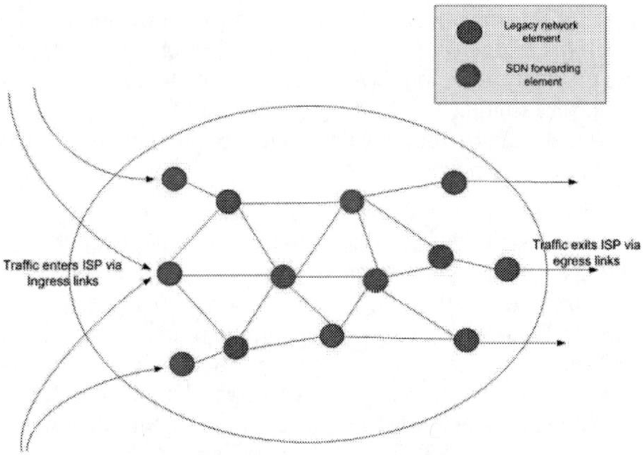

Figure 1. Hybrid Service Provider Network

The flexibility of routing inside the ISP's network is greatly limited by HPR. One possibility to free the ISP from the drawbacks of HPR is the Software-Defined Networking (SDN) paradigm. The purpose of introducing SDN routers into the legacy infrastructure is to make this internal routing less rigid, thereby enabling us to achieve greater load balancing on the egress links.

However, the complete overhaul of an existing ISP network

into an SDN network is an economical, managerial, and technical challenge. To this end, ISPs may choose to transition to SDN in incremental steps, migrating from traditional networks to hybrid networks that are a combination of legacy and SDN routers. An example of such a network is shown in Figure 1. Introducing SDN incrementally reaps the potential benefits of SDN while imposing a smaller economical and managerial cost.

The increase in routing flexibility introduced by SDN will have a positive effect on the redistribution of traffic that must be performed when a legacy router is shutdown. Keeping this in mind, the problem we explore in this paper is to leverage the presence of SDN routers in the legacy network to shutdown as many routers as possible while ensuring that the maximum link utilization (MLU) at the egress links remains less than 100%. The presence of SDN routers ensures that traffic can be distributed more evenly between egress links, since it adds more flexibility to the internal routing decisions, and it allows the possibility of routing traffic over paths that would otherwise not be chosen by an intra-domain routing protocol such as OSPF.

A. *Results and Contributions*

In this paper, we address the problem of minimizing the total power consumed by the network subject to the constraints that the traffic demand is met and that the MLU at the egress links is bounded. The goal is to minimize power consumption by shutting down routers in the network. Both legacy routers and SDN routers may be shutdown. The only restrictions we impose is that ingress routers cannot be shutdown, and a router cannot be shutdown if by doing so the network becomes partitioned.

We formulate the *green hybrid SDN problem*, and we propose a heuristic to choose which routers are to be upgraded with SDN capabilities. We show through simulations that our heuristic outperforms the random selection of routers. That is, carefully selecting which routers are upgraded with SDN increases routing flexibility in such a way that a larger number of routers can be shutdown without exceeding the desired MLU of the egress routers.

The rest of the paper is organized as follows. In Section II, we review related works that independently address the energy efficiency problem in legacy, hybrid, and SDN-only networks. In Section III, we review some background in inter-AS vs intra-AS routing, and also review our earlier work on minimizing egress link utilization in hybrid SDN networks. In Section IV, we present the green hybrid SDN problem, and our heuristics are presented in Section V. Simulation results are presented in Section VI. Concluding remarks are given in Section VII.

II. Related Work

We first review work related to incremental SDN deployment and traffic engineering in hybrid networks. Hybrid SDN networks, in which legacy routers co-exist with SDN nodes, have been an interesting field of study in the SDN community starting with the ideas discussed in [2]. The problem of traffic engineering in a hybrid enterprise network has also been studied in recent years. The first paper to address network performance issues in an incrementally deployed SDN network, [3], explores how SDN can be leveraged to dynamically manage traffic in a hybrid environment.

The traffic engineering (TE) problem in an SDN/OSPF environment is studied in [4], where the goal is to optimize OSPF link weight settings to lower the MLU in the network. Optimizing TE performance over all the network links in a hybrid-SDN environment is studied in [5]. In [6], the maximum flow problem in hybrid SDN networks is explored and an FPTAS is proposed for solving it. Further, [7] focuses on ISP networks with the TE objective of minimizing the MLU over its peering links.

Energy efficiency in ISP networks has been significantly explored in various network scenarios including legacy networks, hybrid SDN networks, and pure SDN networks. We first look at the most relevant studies in the legacy network scenario.

To reduce the total power consumption in a legacy network, numerous studies propose shutting down links and/or entire routers in the network, based on the ideas discussed in [8]. The idea explored in [9] and [10] is to increase energy savings by turning off links and routers in the network subject to QoS constraints such as MLU. In the former, simple heuristics are presented to selectively turn off links and routers while in the latter, a new algorithm based on the power consumption of nodes and links is proposed. The goal in [11] is to shut down cables in bundled links while ensuring that there is enough room to satisfy the traffic demand.

In [12], the authors propose a routing algorithm that precomputes loop-free next-hops for each primary next-hop to effectively detour around links with low traffic load, allowing for traffic aggregation onto links for increased power savings. The study in [13] minimizes energy consumption by turning off unused links in cabled bundles and nodes, while ensuring the traffic demand for each session is satisfied. The authors in [14] present a technique that uses a scalable, online technique to spread the load among multiple paths so as to increase energy savings while achieving the same traffic rates as the energy-oblivious approaches.

In [15], the authors propose a framework that identifies energy critical paths and uses an online TE mechanism to deactivate and activate network elements on demand. [16] proposes a mechanism that maximizes the number of links and/or line-cards that can be put to sleep under constraints such as link utilization and packet delay. This mechanism relies on a centralized controller to make the TE decisions and disseminates the decisions to routers, which then turn on/off line cards and ports as needed. Finally, [17]–[19] are a few other green networking studies in legacy networks.

Next, we briefly go over the energy efficiency research in hybrid SDN networks.

The authors in [20] propose an SDN-based energy-aware routing and resource management model in which the SDN controller uses pre-established multi-paths and performs routing and admission control based on these paths. These paths are turned on/off based on traffic load for energy savings. In [21], the authors propose a hybrid energy-aware TE algorithm which determines the optimal setting for the OSPF link weight and the splitting ratio of SDNs to enable aggregating traffic onto partial links and turning off underutilized links to save energy. [22] focuses on finding the most appropriate percentage of legacy IP nodes to be upgraded to SDN with the goal of putting to sleep links and/or SDN nodes where applicable. The study also gives a selection criterion for selecting SDN nodes to increase energy efficiency of the network. Further, the study in [23] determines the minimum-power network subsets that can satisfy the traffic demand and shuts down unnecessary SDN switches and links.

Studies that focus on energy saving in pure SDN networks include [24]–[28]. The approaches here include modifications/extensions to the OpenFlow protocol and heuristics to aggregate traffic and/or minimize the number of active SDN elements required to satisfy traffic demands.

To the best of our knowledge, our study is the first to take into consideration inter-AS traffic engineering while shutting down nodes in hybrid SDN networks for reducing total energy consumption of the network.

III. Background

We next review some background in inter-AS vs. intra-AS routing, and also our earlier work on minimizing egress link utilization in hybrid SDN networks.

A. Intra-AS vs. Inter-AS Routing

An *autonomous system* (AS) is a group of networks (i.e., IP prefixes) that is controlled by a single administrative entity, such as a university, a company, or an organization. Currently, the Internet has over 80,000 autonomous systems (ASms). Figure 2 shows an AS M that has four neighboring ASms. In this figure, we assume that IP prefix 210.1.0.0/16 is reachable via both ASms A and B (perhaps several AS-hops away), while IP prefixes 200.1.0.0/16 and 220.1.0.0/16 are only reachable via AS A and AS B, respectively.

Border routers exchange prefix reachability information with each other via the BGP protocol. E.g., border router r_1 in AS M learns about IP prefix 210.1.0.0/16 via its neighboring router r_A in AS A, and border router r_B learns about this same prefix via its neighboring router r_B in AS B. It is possible that these IP prefixes are located many AS-hops away from ASms A and B. For the purposes of this paper, we only consider the fact that IP prefixes are being advertised by border routers, and ignore the number of AS-hops to reach them.

We assume that interior routers (i.e., routers not located at the border of the AS) do not speak BGP. This is commonly the case for a medium-sized AS. Thus, interior routers are not aware of the existence of other ASms. They do, however, run an Internal Gateway Protocol (IGP), such as RIP or OPSF, to find a path to every IP prefix available within its own AS.

To allow interior routers to find a path to the external prefixes, such as 210.1.0.0/16, the border routers employ *route redistribution*. That is, border routers advertise the external prefixes over the IGP as if these prefixes belonged to a link directly attached to them. In this way, each internal router can reach an external prefix by following the shortest path to any border router that advertises the prefix. In Figure 2, routers r_1, r_3, r_5 and r_6 will reach prefix 210.1.0.0/16 via neighboring router r_A, while routers r_2 and r_4 will reach this same prefix via neighboring router r_B.

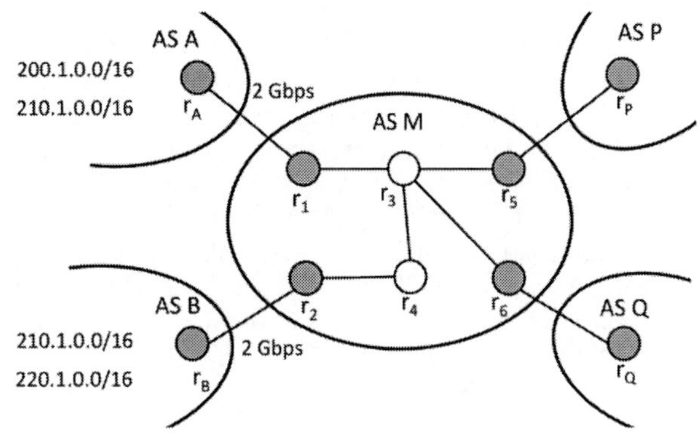

Figure 2. Autonomous systems.

B. Optimizing Egress Link Utilization via Hybrid SDN

As discussed in the next section, shutting down routers will increase the utilization of the egress links. Therefore, finding a method to distribute the traffic evenly over the egress links is beneficial to this problem. Since we assume that the network has SDN routers, we choose to use *SDN Egress Selection* (SES), which we introduced in earlier work [7], to minimize the utilization of egress links. We briefly overview this technique below.

Consider again Figure 2. The links between AS M and its neighbors A and B are labeled with their respective bandwidth, and assume that the IGP uses minimum-hop routing.

Let AS P send 1.5 Gbps to prefix 200.1.0.0/16. This traffic is only advertised by r_1 and thus it must exit via r_1. Let AS Q send 1.5 Gbps to prefix 220.1.0.0/16. Similarly, this must exit via r_2 because only r_2 advertises it. Finally, let each of P and Q send 0.3 Gbps to prefix 210.1.0.0/16. Due to minimum-hop routing, this 0.6 Gbps will exit via r_1, causing this egress link to overflow. Consider now turning a single router into an SDN router, in particular, r_3. This allows r_3 to divert traffic in any way we choose. Let r_3 forward the traffic for prefix 210.1.0.0/16 towards r_1 if it originates from AS P, and towards r_2 (via r_4) if it originates from Q. In this way, both links receive only 1.8 Gbps each, reaching a utilization of 90%.

The SES problem has similarities with the NP-hard problem of minimizing the makespan in unrelated parallel machines [29], [30]. This scheduling problem consists of m parallel machines and n independent jobs, such that, processing job j on machine i requires time $p_{i,j}$. The makespan of a schedule is the maximum total time used by any machine. The objective is to find a schedule that minimizes the makespan. Note that we can map the SES problem to the above scheduling problem by considering each egress link to be a machine, and each traffic flow from an ingress router to a destination prefix to be a job. The processing time of a flow at an egress is set to either the bandwidth of the flow or infinity, depending on whether or not the routing of the flow via minimum-hop routing plus SDN re-routing reaches that egress router.

A 2-approximation solution to the makespan problem is given in [29], [30]. Given the specific nature of the SES problem, we have shown in [7] that the rounding obtains a solution that is very close to optimal, and thus, much smaller than the theoretical bound of twice the optimal.

IV. The Green Hybrid SDN Problem

We consider an AS where each router is either a border router or an interior router. Border routers are divided into two sets: *ingress routers* and *egress routers*. Interior routers are also divided into two sets: *SDN routers* and *legacy routers*. Each egress router r has an egress link of capacity $C(r)$.

A traffic *flow* $f(i,p)$ corresponds to the traffic from ingress router i destined for IP prefix p. Each flow $f(i,p)$ has a *demand*, $D(i,p)$, that corresponds to the amount of traffic of the flow. A traffic flow exits the AS via a single egress router, i.e., we assume that a flow cannot be split among multiple egress routers. For each IP prefix p and egress router e, $avail(e,p)$ is true if and only if e received an advertisement for p from its neighboring AS. Thus, flow $f(i,p)$ can only exit the AS via some egress e where $avail(e,p)$ is true.

A sequence of routers, $r_0, r_1, \ldots, r_n$, is said to be a *hybrid routing path* iff r_0 is an ingress router, r_n is an egress router, and for each r_i, $0 \leq i < n$, r_{i+1} is the next-hop router along the IGP path from r_i to r_n, or r_i is an SDN router whose neighbors include r_{i+1}.

We assume that there exists an SDN controller node that determines the forwarding tables of the SDN routers. The SDN controller is assumed to be aware of the network topology and the paths chosen by the IGP. E.g., the IGP could be OSPF, and the SDN routers forward to it a copy of the link-state advertisements that they receive. The controller is also aware of the traffic matrix either directly from the network operators or via some interaction with the ingress routers.

Our *Green Hybrid SDN problem* is as follows. Consider a legacy AS network, and let R be the set of legacy routers in this network. We are given two upper bounds. The first is an upper bound U on the link utilization on egress links. The second is an upper bound k on the number of legacy routers that will be replaced by SDN routers. The output consists of finding two sets, S and R', such that:

- $R' \subset R$. This set contains the routers that are to be powered down.
- $S \subset R$ and $|S| \leq k$. Each router in S will be replaced by an SDN router.
- For every IP prefix p, every ingress i, and every egress e, the reduced network (i.e., the network consisting of routers in $R - R'$) contains a hybrid routing path from ingress i to an egress e such that $avail(e,p)$ is true.

  Notice that, assuming that every ingress has traffic from at least one prefix, then no ingress router can be part of R'. Egress routers, along with interior routers, may belong to R'.
- The egress MLU is at most U. That is,

  $$\forall e, \ \frac{Load(e)}{C(e)} \leq U \leq 1$$

  Above, $Load(e)$ is the sum of all the traffic demands of flows that are assigned to egress router e.
- The cardinality of R' is the largest possible, i.e., the energy savings is maximized by powering down the largest possible number of routers.

Note that S and R' are not defined to be mutually exclusive. However, if a router r belongs to both sets, then r will be powered down. In this case, the SDN functionality of r is of no use, and its inclusion in S is meaningless. Thus, effectively, S and R' can be thought of as being disjoint.

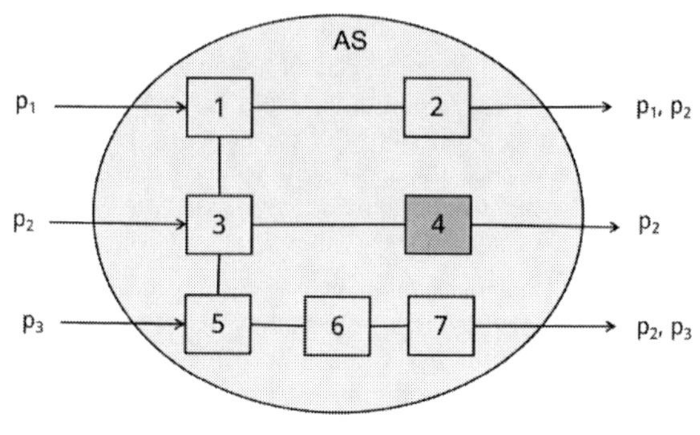

Figure 3. SDN selection example.

As routers are turned off and network paths become unavailable, it is paramount to distribute the traffic evenly among the remaining egress routers. Otherwise, the egress MLU increases beyond the desired bound. As mentioned above, we use the (SES) method that we introduced in [7] to perform this load balancing.

In [7], we assumed that the location of the SDN routers was given as input to the problem. In this paper, however, we assume that that we are free to choose which routers will be upgraded with SDN.

Different choices for set S will yield significantly different cardinalities for set R', and hence, different savings in power. As an example, consider Figure 3, where there is a single AS with three ingress routers, three egress routers, and three prefixes. Note that in light of the IGP, prefixes p_1, p_2, p_3, will exit via egresses 2, 4, and 7, respectively.

Note that 4 is the only router that can be shutdown. This is because the ingress routers cannot be shutdown (otherwise incoming traffic is dropped), and furthermore, each of p_1 and p_3 is available at a single egress, so egress routers 2 and 7 cannot be shutdown either. Finally, 6 cannot be shutdown since otherwise p_3 would not reach its egress. Thus, assume router 4 is shutdown. The IGP would then route traffic for p_2 via egress 2 since it is closer than egress 7.

Assume next that the combined traffic of p_1 and p_2 exceeds the desired utilization of egress 2. However, assume egress 7 can easily handle the combined traffic of p_2 and p_3. Let $k = 1$, i.e., we are only allowed to transform a single router with SDN. The only sensible choice is router 3, which can divert the traffic of p_2 towards 5, and hence, towards egress 7. Any other choice for the SDN router would be unable to affect the traffic, leading to an over-utilization of egress 2, and thus, router 4 would not be allowed to shutdown in this case.

The above example illustrates the importance of the heuristic to select the routers in S. Here, there will be energy savings if and only if the heuristic chooses router 3.

V. Heuristics

We next present several heuristics for selecting set S. Before doing so, we present the overall steps of the method.

1) First, k routers are chosen by one of the heuristics below to be transformed into SDN routers.
2) A router is chosen at random (not including ingresses) and is shutdown.
3) The network is checked to ensure that it is not partitioned, and that there is a hybrid routing path for each flow to an egress router advertising the flow's prefix.
4) The method in [7] is used to see if the SDN nodes can help in routing the traffic in such a way that the egress MLU is at most U.
5) If bound U is not violated, the router is permanently removed from the network.
6) We return to step 2 above. We end when no router can be removed from the network without violating U.

A. Diverting Traffic

For this heuristic, we pick routers that have the ability to "bump" traffic towards any egress other than the IGP-chosen egress, provided the egress is advertising the prefix. To elaborate, let p be an IP prefix, and let $distance(r, e)$ be the IGP distance or cost from router r to egress router e. Also, let $exit(r, p)$ be the egress router through which the traffic from r to p exists the AS. That is,

$$\forall e,\ avail(e, p) \Rightarrow distance(r, exit(r, p)) \leq distance(r, e)$$

Finally, let $path(r, e)$ be the IGP path from router r to egress router e. Then, we say that r is an *SDN candidate* if there is a router s and a prefix p such that: s is a neighbor of r, $exit(r, p) \neq exit(s, p)$, and $r \notin path(s, exit(s, p))$.

Consider the example in Figure 4. Let prefix p be announced by egress routers 9 and 10. Then, for routers 1, 3, 5, and 7, egress 9 is the exit router for prefix p. Similarly, for routers 2, 4, 6, 8, and 11, their exit router is 10. Thus, one SDN candidate is router 3, because $exit(3, p) \neq exit(4, p)$, and 3 is not contained in $path(4, 10)$. Similarly, routers 4, 7, and 8 are also SDN candidates.

On occasions, the number of SDN candidates can be greater than the desired number of SDN routers. If so, we simply choose randomly within the set of candidates.

B. Most Visited

This heuristic is based on the diverting-traffic heuristic. The steps are as follows:

- Apply the diverting traffic heuristic to find the SDN candidate routers.
- Calculate all the IGP paths from each input flow to its egress router.
- Rank the SDN candidate routers according to the number of these IGP paths that cross the candidate router.

For Figure 4, the most-visited heuristic results in choosing routers 4 and 8 first since they both appear in two paths: (2,10) and (11,10). These are followed by 3 and 7 since they are visited by only one path: (1,9).

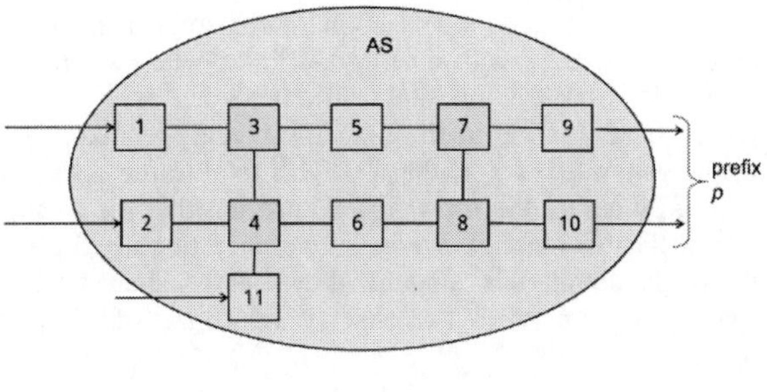

Figure 4. Network example.

C. Degree

This heuristic first identifies SDN candidates as in the diverting traffic heuristic, and the degree of the router is then used to rank the SDN candidates. We arrange routers in decreasing order of their degree. Thus, in Figure 4, router 4 is picked first. This is followed by routers 3, 7, and 8.

D. Most Traffic

For the final heuristic, we assume that we know the pattern of the traffic demand in the network. For each flow, we first calculate the shortest path from its ingress to the closest egress that advertises its prefix, i.e., the path taken by the legacy IGP. We prioritize routers by adding the traffic demands of all the flows that the IGP routes through them. Higher priority is given to those routers that handle the largest amount of traffic.

VI. Simulation Results

We evaluate our heuristics by performing simulations on a Rocketfuel [31] ISP topology with 53 routers and 84 Intra-AS links in the network. Using the Rocketfuel topology information, we conclude that the routers that are not acting as backbone routers are acting as border routers, and we separate these border routers into 14 ingress routers and nine egress routers. We assume that the intra-domain protocol is OSPF, and that the distances are hop-based. Therefore, the shortest path to a destination is the path with the least number of hops.

We generate synthetic traffic flows from each ingress router, where the number of traffic flows through the network is the number of ingress routers times the number of prefixes. We also assume that each ingress router has incoming traffic destined to all the prefix advertised in the network. For example, in the case of 40 prefixes, this would give us 14 $\times$ 40 = 560 traffic flows.

We consider a traffic scenario with 40 prefix advertisements. Typically in an ISP, the number of prefixes in the routing table can scale to large numbers. However, it has been shown that only a small fraction of these prefixes are actually responsible for a major portion of the traffic traversing the ISP network [32]. Generally, a prefix advertisement may be received and advertised by multiple egress routers in the AS. In this paper, we simply choose to advertise each prefix at all the egress border routers.

Each of the egress routers is assumed to connect with the neighboring AS with a single peering link. The capacity of the egress links is set to 1000 scaled units. The total amount of traffic generated is a fraction of the total capacity of the egress links. E.g., with nine egress links, where each link has a capacity of 1000, the total traffic generated is $f \times 1000 \times 9$, where $0 < f < 1$. In the case of six egress links, the total traffic generated is $f \times 1000 \times 6$. This total traffic is distributed randomly across the input flows, ensuring that the total traffic is exactly this amount. We have chosen f to be 0.2. Although relatively small, this amount allows us to shut down many routers in the network and observe the impact of adding SDN routers.

In each of the scenarios, we start with zero SDN routers and increment up to twenty SDN routers. Each point in our plots represents the number of routers that can be turned off averaged over ten simulation runs. Of the heuristics discussed above, the diverting traffic heuristic performed the best. No improvement was seen by adding the most visited refinement nor the degree refinement. For lack of space, we focus on comparing the diverting traffic heuristic against randomly selecting SDN routers.

We begin by presenting the diverting-traffic heuristic in Figures 5, 6 and 7. The number of available egress routers varies from three up to nine. For each of these cases, the bound U on the MLU is varied from 0.7 up to 0.9. This is followed by Figures 8, 9, and 10 with a similar configuration except that the heuristic is just random selection of the SDN routers.

An interesting phenomenon occurs in Figures 5 and 8. Even without SDN routers, having only three egress routers allows us to turn off a total of 29 routers. It appears to suggest that a lower number of egress routers is best. However, this is just a side-effect of how we chose to generate traffic. Recall that the total input traffic generated is $f \times 1000 \times$ (number of egress routers). Thus, the input traffic in the case of only three egress routers is only a third of the input traffic in the case when nine egress routers are available. Thus, as routers are shut down, the nine egress routers case has to squeeze a larger amount of traffic through a smaller number of egress links, and thus, requires a large number of SDN routers to turn off the same number of routers as the case of three egress routers.

Figures 6, 7, 9, and 10, clearly show that as the number of SDN routers in the network is increased, a larger number of routers can be shutdown without violating the link utilization bound. The number of SDN routers need not be large. For example, from Figure 7, with only six SDN routers we are able to shutdown about 23 routers of the maximum 29 possible. No simulation point, regardless of its parameters, was able to shutdown more than 29 routers.

A direct comparison of the diverting traffic vs. random is given in Figure 11. It clearly shows the superiority of the diverting traffic approach over the random approach regardless of the utilization bound chosen.

Finally, Figure 12 shows the diverting-traffic heuristic with $U = 0.75$, and a curve for each of 3, 6, and 9 routers. The figure clearly shows that, for each of these cases, as the number of SDN routers increases, the number of routers that can be shutdown also increases, as desired.

VII. Concluding Remarks

We have introduced the green SDN hybrid problem and evaluated several heuristics for it. Our goal was to ensure

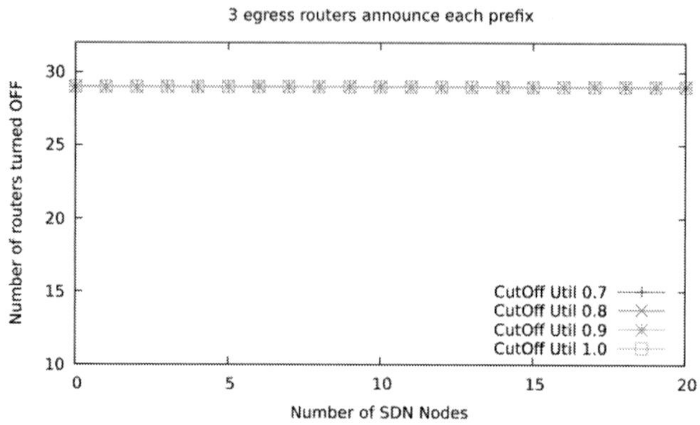

Figure 5. Diverting traffic for three egress routers

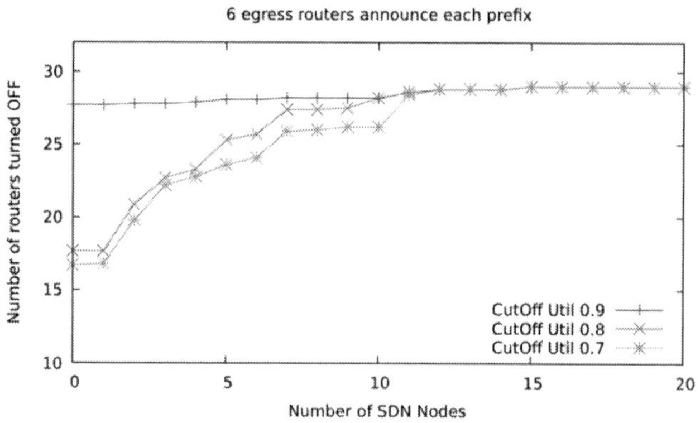

Figure 6. Diverting traffic for six egress routers

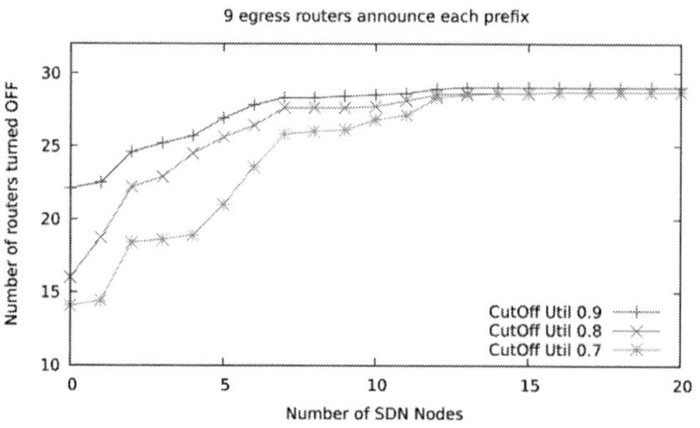

Figure 7. Diverting traffic for nine egress routers

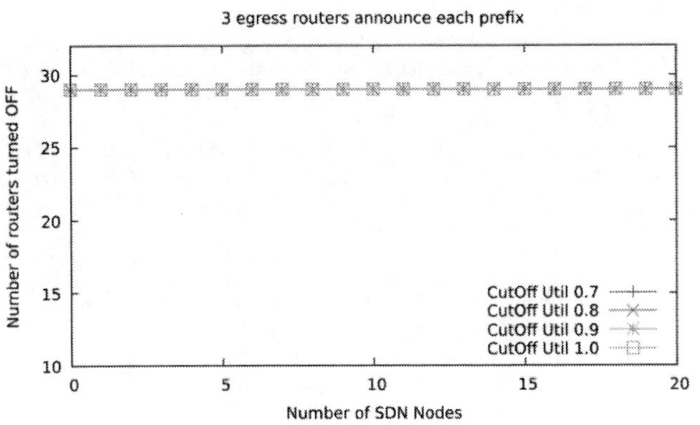

Figure 8. Random placement for three egress routers

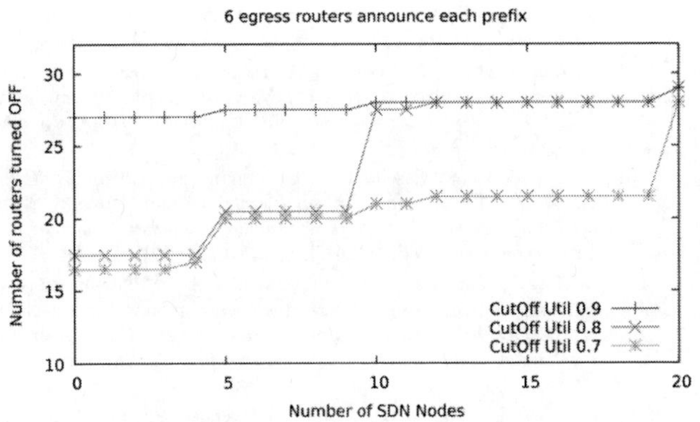

Figure 9. Random placement for six egress routers

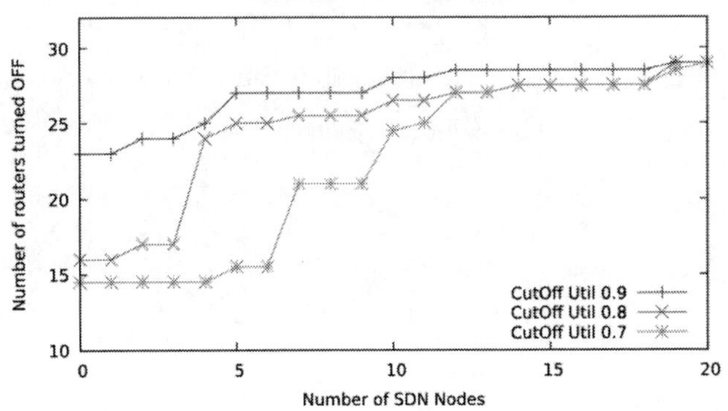

Figure 10. Random placement for nine egress routers

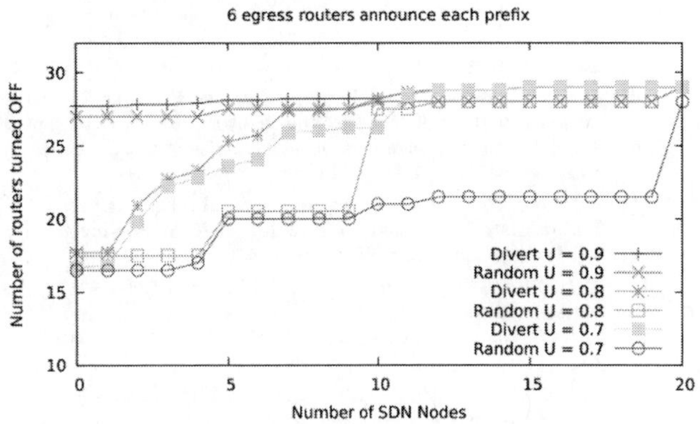

Figure 11. Diverting traffic vs. random placement

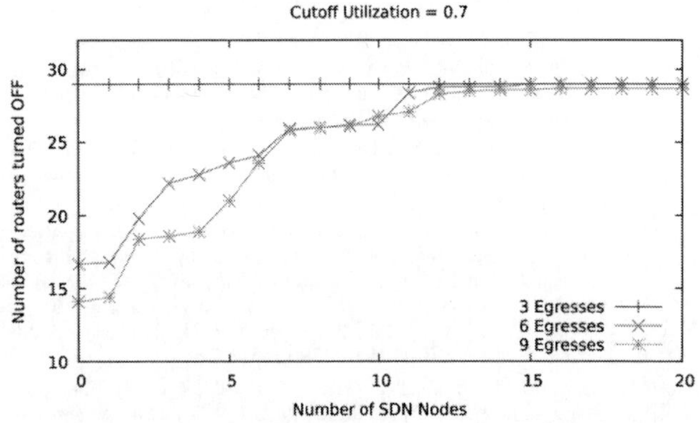

Figure 12. Diverting traffic from three up to nine egress routers

egress links are not over utilized due to the diverting of all the traffic onto a few egress links. We show through our simulations that it is possible to achieve significant energy savings and maintain a bounded link utilization with only a few SDN routers. We also show that in such a hybrid network, the location of the SDN routers play an important role in maximizing energy savings.

There are several directions possible for future work. We plan to continue to investigate various heuristics and apply them to a wide variety of topologies to study their effectiveness. Also, we have assumed that the traffic load is static. If the traffic load changes over time, the SDN controller must recalculate routes and propagate them to the SDN routers. It would be beneficial to come up with a scheme that would allow a smooth transition between the old and new set of routing tables. Finally, we have assumed that all routers consume the same amount of energy, and we have not considered shutting down individual links rather than entire routers. Thus, we also plan to investigate more complex energy models.

REFERENCES

[1] T. Bressoud, R. Rastogi, and M. A. Smith, "Optimal configuration for BGP route selection," in *In Proc. IEEE INFOCOM*, 2003.

[2] D. Levin, M. Canini, S. Schmid, a. feldmann, and f. schaffert, "Panopticon: Reaping the benefits of incremental sdn deployment in enterprise networks," in *USENIX Annual Technical Conference*, 2014.

[3] S. Agarwal, M. Kodialam, and T. V. Lakshman, "Traffic engineering in software defined networks," in *2013 Proceedings IEEE INFOCOM*, 2013, pp. 2211–2219.

[4] Y. Guo, Z. Wang, X. Yin, X. Shi, J. Wu, and H. Zhang, "Incremental deployment for traffic engineering in hybrid sdn network," in *2015 IEEE 34th International Performance Computing and Communications Conference (IPCCC)*, Dec 2015, pp. 1–8.

[5] J. He and W. Song, "Achieving near-optimal traffic engineering in hybrid software defined networks," in *2015 IFIP Networking Conference (IFIP Networking)*, May 2015, pp. 1–9.

[6] Y. Hu, W. Wang, X. Gong, X. Que, Y. Ma, and S. Cheng, "Maximizing network utilization in hybrid software-defined networks," in *2015 IEEE Global Communications Conference (GLOBECOM)*, Dec 2015, pp. 1–6.

[7] K. P. Kadiyala and J. A. Cobb, "Inter-as traffic engineering with sdn," in *2017 IEEE Conference on Network Function Virtualization and Software Defined Networks (NFV-SDN)*, Nov 2017, pp. 1–7.

[8] M. Gupta and S. Singh, "Greening of the internet," in *Proceedings of the 2003 Conference on Applications, Technologies, Architectures, and Protocols for Computer Communications*, ser. SIGCOMM '03. New York, NY, USA: ACM, 2003, pp. 19–26. [Online]. Available: http://doi.acm.org/10.1145/863955.863959

[9] L. Chiaraviglio, M. Mellia, and F. Neri, "Reducing power consumption in backbone networks," in *2009 IEEE International Conference on Communications*, June 2009, pp. 1–6.

[10] ——, "Energy-aware backbone networks: A case study," in *2009 IEEE International Conference on Communications Workshops*, June 2009, pp. 1–5.

[11] W. Fisher, M. Suchara, and J. Rexford, "Greening backbone networks: Reducing energy consumption by shutting off cables in bundled links," in *Proceedings of the First ACM SIGCOMM Workshop on Green Networking*, ser. Green Networking '10. New York, NY, USA: ACM, 2010, pp. 29–34. [Online]. Available: http://doi.acm.org/10.1145/1851290.1851297

[12] Q. Li, M. Xu, Y. Yang, L. Gao, Y. Cui, and J. Wu, "Safe and practical energy-efficient detour routing in ip networks," *IEEE/ACM Transactions on Networking*, vol. 22, no. 6, pp. 1925–1937, Dec 2014.

[13] B. Mumey, J. Tang, and S. Hashimoto, "Enabling green networking with a power down approach," in *2012 IEEE International Conference on Communications (ICC)*, June 2012, pp. 2867–2871.

[14] N. Vasić and D. Kostić, "Energy-aware traffic engineering," in *Proceedings of the 1st International Conference on Energy-Efficient Computing and Networking*, ser. e-Energy '10. New York, NY, USA: ACM, 2010, pp. 169–178. [Online]. Available: http://doi.acm.org/10.1145/1791314.1791341

[15] N. Vasić, P. Bhurat, D. Novaković, M. Canini, S. Shekhar, and D. Kostić, "Identifying and using energy-critical paths," in *Proceedings of the Seventh COnference on Emerging Networking EXperiments and Technologies*, ser. CoNEXT '11. New York, NY, USA: ACM, 2011, pp. 18:1–18:12. [Online]. Available: http://doi.acm.org/10.1145/2079296.2079314

[16] M. Zhang, C. Yi, B. Liu, and B. Zhang, "Greente: Power-aware traffic engineering," in *Proceedings of the The 18th IEEE International Conference on Network Protocols*, ser. ICNP '10. Washington, DC, USA: IEEE Computer Society, 2010, pp. 21–30. [Online]. Available: http://dx.doi.org/10.1109/ICNP.2010.5762751

[17] A. Cianfrani, V. Eramo, M. Listanti, M. Marazza, and E. Vittorini, "An energy saving routing algorithm for a green ospf protocol," in *2010 INFOCOM IEEE Conference on Computer Communications Workshops*, March 2010, pp. 1–5.

[18] O. Okonor, N. Wang, Z. Sun, and S. Georgoulas, "Link sleeping and wake-up optimization for energy aware isp networks," in *2014 IEEE Symposium on Computers and Communications (ISCC)*, June 2014, pp. 1–7.

[19] R. Bolla, R. Bruschi, A. Cianfrani, and M. Listanti, "Enabling backbone networks to sleep," *Netwrk. Mag. of Global Internetwkg.*, vol. 25, no. 2, pp. 26–31, Mar. 2011. [Online]. Available: http://dx.doi.org/10.1109/MNET.2011.5730525

[20] M. R. Celenlioglu, S. B. Goger, and H. A. Mantar, "An sdn-based energy-aware routing model for intra-domain networks," in *22nd International Conference on Software, Telecommunications and Computer Networks (SoftCOM)*, Sept 2014, pp. 61–66.

[21] Y. Wei, X. Zhang, L. Xie, and S. Leng, "Energy-aware traffic engineering in hybrid sdn/ip backbone networks," *Journal of Communications and Networks*, vol. 18, no. 4, pp. 559–566, Aug 2016.

[22] J. Galn-Jimnez, "Legacy ip-upgraded sdn nodes tradeoff in energy-efficient hybrid ip/sdn networks," *Comput. Commun.*, vol. 114, no. C, pp. 106–123, dec 2017. [Online]. Available: https://doi.org/10.1016/j.comcom.2017.10.010

[23] H. Wang, Y. Li, D. Jin, P. Hui, and J. Wu, "Saving energy in partially deployed software defined networks," *IEEE Transactions on Computers*, vol. 65, no. 5, pp. 1578–1592, May 2016.

[24] R. Bolla, R. Bruschi, F. Davoli, and C. Lombardo, "Fine-grained energy-efficient consolidation in sdn networks and devices," *IEEE Transactions on Network and Service Management*, vol. 12, pp. 132–145, 2015.

[25] A. Markiewicz, P. N. Tran, and A. Timm-Giel, "Energy consumption optimization for software defined networks considering dynamic traffic," *IEEE 3rd International Conference on Cloud Networking (CloudNet)*, pp. 155–160, 2014.

[26] S. S. Tadesse, C. Casetti, C.-F. Chiasserini, and G. Landi, "Energy-efficient traffic allocation in sdn-basec backhaul networks: Theory and implementation," *14th IEEE Annual Consumer Communications Networking Conference (CCNC)*, pp. 209–215, 2017.

[27] S. Oda, D. Nobayashi, Y. Fukuda, and T. Ikenaga, "Flow-based routing schemes for minimizing network energy consumption using openflow," in *The Fourth International Conference on Smart Grids, Green Communications and IT Energy-aware Technologies (ENERGY 2014)*, April 2014.

[28] H. Ying, L. Tao, B. N. C., and W. Wenjie, "An initial load-based green software defined network," *Applied Sciences*, vol. 7, no. 5, 2017. [Online]. Available: http://www.mdpi.com/2076-3417/7/5/459

[29] J. K. Lenstra, D. B. Shmoys, and E. Tardos, "Approximation algorithms for scheduling unrelated parallel machines," in *Foundations of Computer Science, 1987., 28th Annual Symposium on*. IEEE, 1987, pp. 217–224.

[30] D. Du, K.-I. Ko, and X. Hu, *Design and Analysis of Approximation Algorithms*. New York, NY: Springer, 2012.

[31] N. Spring, R. Mahajan, D. Wetherall, and T. Anderson, "Measuring isp topologies with rocketfuel," *IEEE/ACM Trans. Netw.*, pp. 2–16, feb 2004.

[32] N. Feamster, J. Borkenhagen, and J. Rexford, "Guidelines for interdomain traffic engineering," in *ACM SIGCOMM Computer Communication Review*, October 2003, pp. 19–30.

Comparative Evaluation of Database Performance in an Internet of Things Context

Denis Arnst*, Valentin Plenk†, Adrian Wöltche‡
Institute of Information Systems at Hof University, Hof, Germany
Email: *denis.arnst@iisys.de, †valentin.plenk@iisys.de, ‡adrian.woeltche@iisys.de

Abstract—**We use an application scenario that collects, transports and stores sensor data in a database. The data is gathered with a high frequency of 1000 datasets per second. In the context of this scenario, we analyze the performance of multiple popular database systems. The benchmark results include the load on the system writing the data and the system running the database.**

Keywords–performance; benchmark; nosql; relational; database; industry 4.0; mariadb; mongodb; influxdb; internet of things; high frequency data acquisition; time series.

I. Introduction

Recently popular media are heralding the advent of a new age with buzzwords like "Internet of Things" (IoT) or "Industry 4.0" (I4.0). One of the popular mantras is "data is the new oil". This claim is surely true for applications like predictive maintenance where data gathered during operation of a production machine is mined for wear indicators. Many papers address the "refining process" (e.g. [1]–[3]) and propose data-mining algorithms that extract said indicators from a database or a data lake.

In this paper, however, we focus on collecting and storing time series data as integral part of the industrial data analytics process [4]. This can be very challenging both in terms of engineering the instrumentation and in implementing fast data-acquisition and data-handling software. In one of our research projects, we collect and store $\approx 4\frac{\text{GB}}{\text{day}}$.

Standard databases can be tuned towards high performance reading or writing of data, but often not towards both at once. Especially when a fast retrieval of time series data is of interest, for example in predictive analytics, relational databases rely on B-tree indexes that permit a fast search for data. These indexes are a huge performance bottleneck if frequent updates are made. This stems from B-trees being optimized for random fills and not for updates only coming from one side of the tree. [5] propose structures like the B(x)-tree to overcome this problem. Nevertheless, standard databases do not implement specialized index structures in most cases. Instead, specialized "time-series" databases for this use case exists (e.g. [6]–[9]).

To verify whether these databases are more suitable for our application, we use the benchmark scenario presented in Section II that generates a standard load on all subsystems of the setup, to compare relational, NoSQL and specialized time-series databases. Section III presents our test candidates.

In Section IV, we describe the different implementations we developed for writing to the databases. We evaluated several ideas from [10], such as time series grouping.

To evaluate the database performance we measure the load on the involved infrastructural components, i.e., CPU, memory, network and hard disk, and perform the benchmarking, as described in Section V. Section VI discusses our findings. Section VII summarizes the paper and gives a brief outlook on our future work.

Figure 1. The test setup

II. Benchmark Application

One of our currrent projects is using predictive maintenance for analyzing data stemming from a complex tool operating within an industrial machine. The tool is equipped with 13 analog and 37 digital sensors recording mechanical parameters during operation of the tool. The machine tool opens and closes the tool $\approx$ 3 times per second, i.e., 3 working cycles per second. Our application records ≈ 300 samples per cycle from the sensors and stores them in a database for later analysis.

For the tests in this paper, we substitute tool and machine tool with electronic function generators as shown in Figure 1. One function generator is set to make a sinus wave. It is wired to a divider circuit, which accepts one input and divides it into four outputs of different amplitudes. The other generator creates a sawtooth wave. The resulting five analog outputs are wired to GPIO-Inputs of a STM32F4-Discovery board.

In total, we sample 5 analog channels with a resolution of 12 Bit (represented using 2 bytes) and a sample rate of $1000\frac{\text{samples}}{\text{sec}}$. This corresponds to a data rate of $10,000\frac{\text{bytes}}{\text{sec}}$.

Figure 2 shows the flow of the data through our setup. The sensor data is gathered by a microcontroller which sends it to a single board computer via a parallel interface. The single board computer is running two separate applications: one reads from the parallel interface and adds a timestamp to the sensor data. The second application receives the data and writes it to the database on our server. These applications are linked via a Linux message queue. If the second application is not reading fast enough to keep the buffered data in the queue below $\approx 16\text{kByte}$ data is lost.

We use a STM32F407 on a STM32F4Discovery evaluation board to convert the sensor data from analog to digital. The

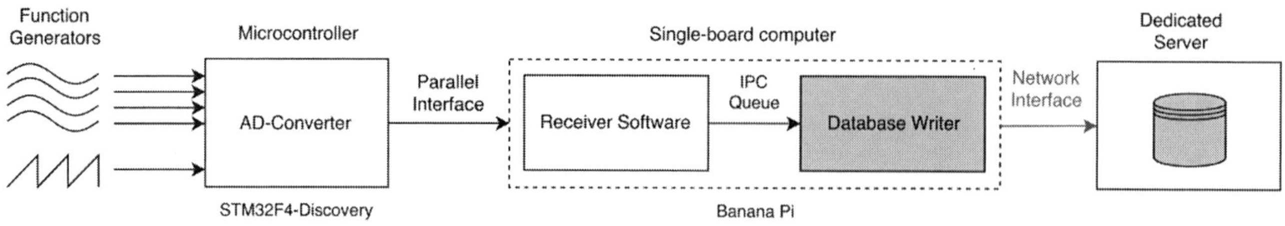

Figure 2. Block diagram of the test setup

embedded application is written in C and does not use any operating system.

The Single-board-Computer is a Banana Pi M3 running the Linux distribution CentOS 7 without an X.Org-Server. This system uses an ARM Cortex A7 Octa-Core with 2 GB RAM and has GigaBit Ethernet on board. The two applications running on this system are written in C and C++.

The database is run on a dedicated server running Linux with an AMD Phenom(tm) II X6 1055T Processor, 16GB RAM (4 x 4GB, DDR3, 1333 MHz) and a 128GB SSD running on a ASRock 880G Extreme 3 mainboard. It also runs CentOS 7 as distribution.

Banana Pi and server are linked via fast ethernet.

The parts of Figure 2 shown with gray background are database specific. We use high-level libraries to access the database and provide three different implementations and server installations.

III. Choice of Databases

Various publications like [7] or [11] list an huge number of different databases. They distinguish three categories: Relational Database Management Systems (RDBMS), NoSQL Database Management Systems (DBMS), and the more specialized Time Series Databases (TSDB). For our benchmark, we chose one system for each category. For the selection we focus on mature (stable releases available for at least 3 years) and free software with options for enterprise support. We mainly consulted the database ranking website [11] as basis for selecting databases for our comparison.

As a representative RDBMS we selected the open source database MariaDB [12]. It is a fork of the popular MySQL database and widely used in Web-Applications and relational scenarios. [13] lists MySQL and its more recent fork MariaDB combined as top RDBMS.

We selected MongoDB [14] as a DBMS advertised expressly for its usefulness in an IoT context with a lot of sensor data. It is also the most promising document store [15].

As TSDB we chose InfluxDB [16] which claims to be highly specialized in sensor data. This claim is confirmed by the score in [17].

IV. The different Implementations

Every millisecond the Database Writer application running on the single-board computer receives a new datapoint. Listing 1 shows the structure of the datapoint: It contains a timestamp and a set of five analog values. The timestamp has a resolution of one nanosecond and uses 12 bytes of memory. The analog values are represented as 16-bit integers. Thus one datapoint uses 22 bytes of memory.

Depending on the architecture of the database, we implemented different ways of storing the data detailed in the following sections. Each implementation itself is optimized concerning runtime complexity for reduced influence on the benchmarks by using memory usage techniques (i.e. stack memory allocation), database specific techniques (i.e. prepared statements), and general algorithmic design principles. This way, we are able to receive optimal database performance results. It is, however, possible, that non-optimized client implementations negatively impact the throughput. This is not covered by this paper for now.

A. *MariaDB – Individual datapoints*

This is a straightforward maybe even naive implementation of the data structure. We sequentially store each datapoint in the database. This results in a high rate of operations on the database ($5000\frac{\text{writes}}{\text{second}}$). Table I shows the structure of the data. A compound index is set on *second* and *nanosecond*. *number* describes the index of the sensor, *measurement* the corresponding sensor value.

TABLE I
MariaDB - Table structure of individual datapoints

Field	Type
second	bigint(20)
nanosecond	int(11)
number	smallint(5) unsigned
measurement	smallint(5) unsigned

Our implementation of the algorithm based on `libmariadb` uses prepared statements and struct data binding for higher performance. Our performance optimizations because of the creation of tables and the explicit transaction preparation and commitment make the MariaDB code the largest and most complicated of all our implementations.

B. *MariaDB – Bulk Datapoints*

This implementation collects all data from one machine cycle at once (in our test scenario: one cycle per second)

Listing 1. One datapoint

```
struct data_point
{
  int64_t s;
  int32_t ns;
  uint16_t measurements[5];
};
```

and writes out one row per cycle. Therefore, we can store the data in bigger units, which reduces the load dramatically. In MariaDB, the JSON field is an alias for longtext field. Yet, the specialized JSON query commands in MariaDB work for such fields, which allows to later query the denormalized data saved. Table II shows the used structure. *second* is an index, *measurements* contains a JSON document built according to the example in Listing 2. The document contains the measurements and its time in nanoseconds in relation to the second of the table. Thus, the rate of index updates is reduced to 1 per second.

TABLE II
MARIADB - TABLE STRUCTURE OF DATAPOINTS IN BULK

Field	Type
second	bigint(20)
size	int(10) unsigned
measurements	json

Listing 2. MariaDB - JSON Documents

```
{
 "measurements": [
   {"ns":346851124,"m":[389,792,1202,315,552]}
   ,{"ns":346933204,"m":[516,794,634,317,559]}
   ...
]}
```

The difficulty of this adaption is similar to the original ”naive” approach , but in one detail even more complicated: As it is theoretically impossible to know how many measurements one cycle will have (most of the time the stated 5000 measurements per second in our case, but this is not guaranteed), we needed to implement a dynamically growing character field for the JSON data. We also needed to change the struct binding in the transaction commitment for honoring the dynamical length of the JSON data.

C. MongoDB – Individual Datapoints

As a document-orientated database, MongoDB allows for flexible schemata. Data is organized internally in BSON (Binary JSON) documents, which are in turn grouped in collections.

Saving the individual datapoints according to Listing 1 each measurement would be a document with the time of measurement and the values organized as a JSON-array.

The database supports setting an index on a field of a document. To support further searching of measurements, an index is set on time. With such a structure, numerous documents are created per second. After each document, the index needs to be updated, which results in high computational effort.

The software for the MongoDB Database Writer is written in C++ and uses `mongocxx` in conjunction with the `bsoncxx` library. The document orientated approach of MongoDB makes designing data structures very flexible. However, the freedom leads to more work on the initial programming approach. Also the need to link two libraries creates additional effort.

D. MongoDB – Bulk Datapoints

As stated in Section IV-B we can store a bigger number of datapoints at once. In MongoDB, we can implement this with the structure shown in Listing 3.

Listing 3. Datapoints in bulk

```
{
  "time" : ISODate("2018-02-12T19:56:49Z"),
  "measurements" : [
    { "time" : ISODate("2018-02-12T19:56:49.135Z"), "sensors" : [ 0, 0, 0, 9, 347 ] }
    ,
    { "time" : ISODate("2018-02-12T19:56:49.136Z"), "sensors" : [ 0, 2, 4, 10, 351 ]
    },
    ...
  ]
}
```

The time value of the top-level document has a precision of a second. This document holds all datapoints sampled during this second in an array. Every nested document contains the exact time of its measurement and the actual sensor-values. With this approach, the index has to be updated only once per second resulting in optimized write performance. Nevertheless, it must be considered that in this case only a whole second but no parts of it can be retrieved efficiently. However, because of the high increase in write throughput, we accept this drawback.

The application creates a document for a whole second and fills it until the second has passed. Accordingly one such document is inserted per second.

The documentation for MongoDB provides examples for the use of streams and basic builders consisting of function calls. Yet the use of nested structures and the nature of C++-streams is poorly documented in the doxygen-based manuals, increasing the implementation effort.

E. InfluxDB

As a time-series database InfluxDB has a strict schema design. Every series of data consists of points. Each point has a timestamp, the name of the measurement, an optional tag, and one or more key-values fields. Timestamps have an accuracy of up to one nanosecond and are indexed. The name of the measurement should describe the data stored. The optional tags are also indexed and used for grouping data. Data is retrieved with InfluxQL, a SQL-like query language. Data is written using the InfluxDB line-protocol (Listing 4). The first string is the name of the measurement, here simply *measurement*. Subsequently following the key-values with five measurements and finally a timestamp in nanosecond precision.

Listing 4. InfluxDB Line-Protocol example

```
measurement m0=0, m1=0, m2=0, m3=9, m4=347
   1518465409001000000
```

The Database Writer for InfluxDB is written in C. The default API for InfluxDB is HTTP. For our high-frequency write access however, we haven chosen the UDP protocol which is also supported. In this case, the data is composed into a line-protocol with simple C-String functions and sent with the Unix function `sendto`. Since no external code is required and a custom design of the data structure is not possible, using the database is straight-forward and fast to implement.

Additionally, InfluxDB also offers built-in functions to process data statistically and a client library is not necessary, which is a benefit for software developers using it.

The choice of UDP has the probability of data loss, which is acceptable in our use case. For enabling the UDP service of InfluxDB, the OS was configured correspondingly to the information provided by InfluxData [18].

V. Testing

Most applications in our context face limitations in terms of computing power and network bandwidth. Consequently we measure the load on the single board computer, the load on the server and the network load.

The system load on both computers is measured in terms of CPU and memory usage. We created a script, which runs the specified application for one hour. Before it ends the application, it uses two Linux-System commands to gather the following parameters.

L_{CPU} indicates the processor usage. We obtain this value with the Linux command `ps -p` <pid> `-o %cpu` which will return a measure for the percentage of time the process <pid> spent running over the measurement time.

The maximum value for one core is always 100%. On our 8 core single-board computer the absolute maximum value would be $L_{CPU} = 800\%$. On the server the absolute maximum value is 600%.

L_{mem} indicates memory usage in kByte. We use the amount of memory used by the process <pid> as the sum of active and paged memory as returned by the command `ps aux -y | awk '{if ($2 ==` <pid> `) print $6}'`. It outputs the *resident set size* (RSS) memory, the actual memory used which is held in RAM.

L_{disk} shows the the amount of disk used by a database. To determine this parameter we first empty the respective database completely by removing its data folder. Also, we start the database and measure the disk space of the folder before we test. After the test we measure the used disk space again and use the difference as result. `du -sh` <foldername> is used to get the disk consumption of the respective data folder. To put the results in perspective: Our benchmark application gathers and transmits $\approx 53\text{MByte}$ of raw data during the one hour of our test.

L_{IO} shows the average disk input output in $\frac{\text{kb}}{\text{s}}$ caused by the database writing operation. This was measured via `pidstat` command.

L_{net} shows the average bandwidth used. We obtain that value with the command `nload`. We run our test in the university network and therefore have additional external network load. However before each test, we observed the additional network load and as it was always smaller than $1\frac{\text{kbytes}}{\text{sec}}$, we neglected it.

To put L_{IO} and L_{net} in perspective: In our benchmark we transfer $10.000\frac{\text{bytes}}{\text{sec}}$ from the microcontroller to the single-board computer.

Before each test, we restart both the Banana Pi and the server. We then erase the database folder on the server and give both systems $\approx 5\text{min}$ to settle. Then we turn on the function generators, log in to the single-board computer and start the Database Writer software for the currently active database. The actual benchmark begins with starting the Receiver Software.

We let the system gather data from the function generators for 60 minutes. The performance data detailed in Section V is gathered by two scripts running on the single-board computer and the server during the test.

VI. Results

Table IV shows our results. Figure 3 visualizes the data in relation to the maximum values in respective to each criterion.

The Bulk implementations of MariaDB and MongoDB are able to surpass all other databases in regard to server processor usage. InfluxDB required the least CPU usage when only regarding individual implementations. All implementations could handle the high data rate, however the rate of the MariaDB individual implementation was fluctuating in tests. RAM usage of the InfluxDB components were the lowest. Nonetheless, even the utilization of MariaDB - the database with the highest memory usage - was absolutely seen so low that it may not be relevant. The usage and activity of the disk was significantly higher when using MariaDB compared to the others. InfluxDB and the bulk implementation of MongoDB got by with the least amount of disk usage.

To directly compare all our candidates we calculate a combined score by weighing the parameters. In a first step we set the values of each column in Table IV in relation to the columns maximum, so that we compare the relative performance. In the next step, before we add them up, we assign each parameter a weighting.

Since we find that the CPU is the most important parameter, we give it a weight of 2 on server and as resources on client are limited it is weighted with 2.5 there. In absolute terms, the RAM usage on server and client was very little and therefore we weight it with 0.25. For IO we used a SSD, when using a HDD, IO usage could pose a larger problem and therefore it is weighted with 2.5. As the disk usage is already correlating with IO, we weight it with 0.5 so that the impact of the disk results is in a decent relation to the other component results. On difficult places, network-bandwidth could be limited, potentially a data logging application could be connected wirelessly, so we weight it with 1.5.

Lastly we take the subjective difficulty of our implementations into account. We grade on a scale from 5, most difficult to 1 easy and weigh this parameter with 0.2. The individual rating is determined by the explained experience with the client implementation described in Section IV.

The weights are multiplied with each criterion and aggregated, resulting in points. High point values indicate high resource usage according to weighting. For scoring we "invert" the points with the formula

$$Score = max(Points) - Points$$

and normalize the scores relative to the maximum score.

Figure 4 shows the scores without aggregation, where the components forming the final results are outlined. For the final ranking shown in Table III we aggregated all scores by adding the non normalized values.

TABLE III
SCORED RANKING

Implementation	Rank	Score
MariaDB – bulk	1	73
MongoDB – bulk	2	70
InfluxDB	3	64
MongoDB – individual	4	54
MariaDB – individual	5	3

VII. CONCLUSION AND FUTURE WORK

Generally speaking, MongoDB is a good choice. Due to the open structure, additional information can also be stored if required and it performs quite well on both implementations.

However, the optimized MariaDB implementation that saves data in bulks ranks first, as it consumed the least amount of CPU and network.

On the contrary, if a saving of individual values is desired, MariaDB is the last one and InfluxDB is the best in this case.

Our ranking is weighted after the use case described in Section II. When IO is much more important than CPU, MariaDB is potentially lesser ranked, as it had the most IO usage in both implementations.

The paper only covered the writing of databases. Later on, we want to measure the reading and querying performance in another paper. By ensuring that each database uses an index for time, we have already established a good basis for it. Nevertheless, we expect different winners in each test category for the readings.

REFERENCES

[1] D. Wang, J. Liu, and R. Srinivasan, "Data-driven soft sensor approach for quality prediction in a refining process," IEEE Transactions on Industrial Informatics, vol. 6, no. 1, Feb 2010, pp. 11–17, URL: https://dx.doi.org/10.1109/TII.2009.2025124 [retrieved: 2018-08-14].

[2] G. Köksal, İ. Batmaz, and M. C. Testik, "A review of data mining applications for quality improvement in manufacturing industry," Expert Systems with Applications, vol. 38, no. 10, 2011, pp. 13 448 – 13 467, URL: http://www.sciencedirect.com/science/article/pii/S0957417411005793 [retrieved: 2018-08-14].

[3] F. Chen, P. Deng, J. Wan, D. Zhang, A. V. Vasilakos, and X. Rong, "Data mining for the internet of things: Literature review and challenges," International Journal of Distributed Sensor Networks, vol. 11, no. 8, 2015, p. 431047, URL: https://doi.org/10.1155/2015/431047 [retrieved: 2018-08-14].

[4] J. Lee, H. D. Ardakani, S. Yang, and B. Bagheri, "Industrial big data analytics and cyber-physical systems for future maintenance & service innovation," Procedia CIRP, vol. 38, 2015, pp. 3 – 7, proceedings of the 4th International Conference on Through-life Engineering Services.

[5] C. S. Jensen, D. Lin, and B. C. Ooi, "Query and update efficient b+-tree based indexing of moving objects," in Proceedings of the Thirtieth International Conference on Very Large Data Bases - Volume 30, ser. VLDB '04. VLDB Endowment, 2004, pp. 768–779, URL: http://dl.acm.org/citation.cfm?id=1316689.1316756 [retrieved: 2018-08-14].

[6] S. Acreman, "Top 10 time series databases," URL: https://blog.outlyer.com/top10-open-source-time-series-databases [retrieved: 2018-08-14].

[7] A. Bader, O. Kopp, and M. Falkenthal, "Survey and Comparison of Open Source Time Series Databases," Datenbanksysteme für Business, Technologie und Web - Workshopband, 2017, pp. 249 – 268, URL: http://btw2017.informatik.uni-stuttgart.de/slidesandpapers/E4-14-109/paper_web.pdf [retrieved: 2018-08-14].

[8] D. Namiot, "Time series databases," in DAMDID/RCDL, 2015, URL: https://www.semanticscholar.org/paper/Time-Series-Databases-Namiot/bf265b6ee45d814b3acb29fb52b57fd8dbf94ab6 [retrieved: 2018-08-14].

[9] S. Y. Syeda Noor Zehra Naqvi, "Time series databases and influxdb," Studienarbeit, Université Libre de Bruxelles, 2017, URL: http://cs.ulb.ac.be/public/_media/teaching/influxdb_2017.pdf [retrieved: 2018-08-14].

[10] A. M. Castillejos, "Management of time series data," Dissertation, School of Information Sciences and Engineering, 2006, URL: http://www.canberra.edu.au/researchrepository/file/82315cf7-7446-fcf2-6115-b94fbd7599c6/1/full_text.pdf [retrieved: 2018-08-14].

[11] solidIT consulting & software development gmbh, "DB-Engines Ranking," URL: https://db-engines.com/en/ranking [retrieved: 2018-08-14].

[12] "MariaDB homepage," URL: https://mariadb.org/ [retrieved: 2018-08-14].

[13] solidIT consulting & software development gmbh, "DB-Engines Ranking of Relational DBMS," URL: https://db-engines.com/en/ranking/relational+dbms [retrieved: 2018-08-14].

[14] "MongoDB homepage," URL: https://www.mongodb.com/what-is-mongodb [retrieved: 2018-08-14].

[15] solidIT consulting & software development gmbh, "DB-Engines Ranking of Document Stores," URL: https://db-engines.com/en/ranking/document+store [retrieved: 2018-08-14].

[16] "InfluxDB homepage," URL: https://www.influxdata.com/time-series-platform/influxdb/ [retrieved: 2018-08-14].

[17] solidIT consulting & software development gmbh, "DB-Engines Ranking of Time Series DBMS," URL: https://db-engines.com/en/ranking/time+series+dbms [retrieved: 2018-08-14].

[18] "UDP Configuration of InfluxDB," URL: https://github.com/influxdata/influxdb/tree/master/services/udp [retrieved: 2018-08-14].

TABLE IV
TEST RESULTS

	L_{CPU_S}	L_{mem_S}	L_{CPU_C}	L_{mem_C}	L_{io}	L_{disk}	L_{net}	Difficulty
MariaDB – individual	36.6 %	201 kB	7 %	7.8 kB	7396 kB/s	1.27 GB	1.41 Mbit/s	5 (Very high)
MariaDB – bulk	0.6 %	172 kB	2.2 %	8 kB	378 kB/s	240 MB	0.37 Mbit/s	
MongoDB – individual	3 %	758 kB	6.6 %	12 kB	117 kB/s	204 MB	0.78 Mbit/s	4 (high)
MongoDB – bulk	1 %	209 kB	3 %	12 kB	56 kB/s	86 MB	0.63 Mbit/s	
InfluxDB	15.4 %	178 kB	4.9 %	2 kB	81 kB/s	89 MB	0.87 Mbit/s	1 (Very low)
Weight	2	0.25	2.5	0.25	2.5	0.5	1.5	0.2

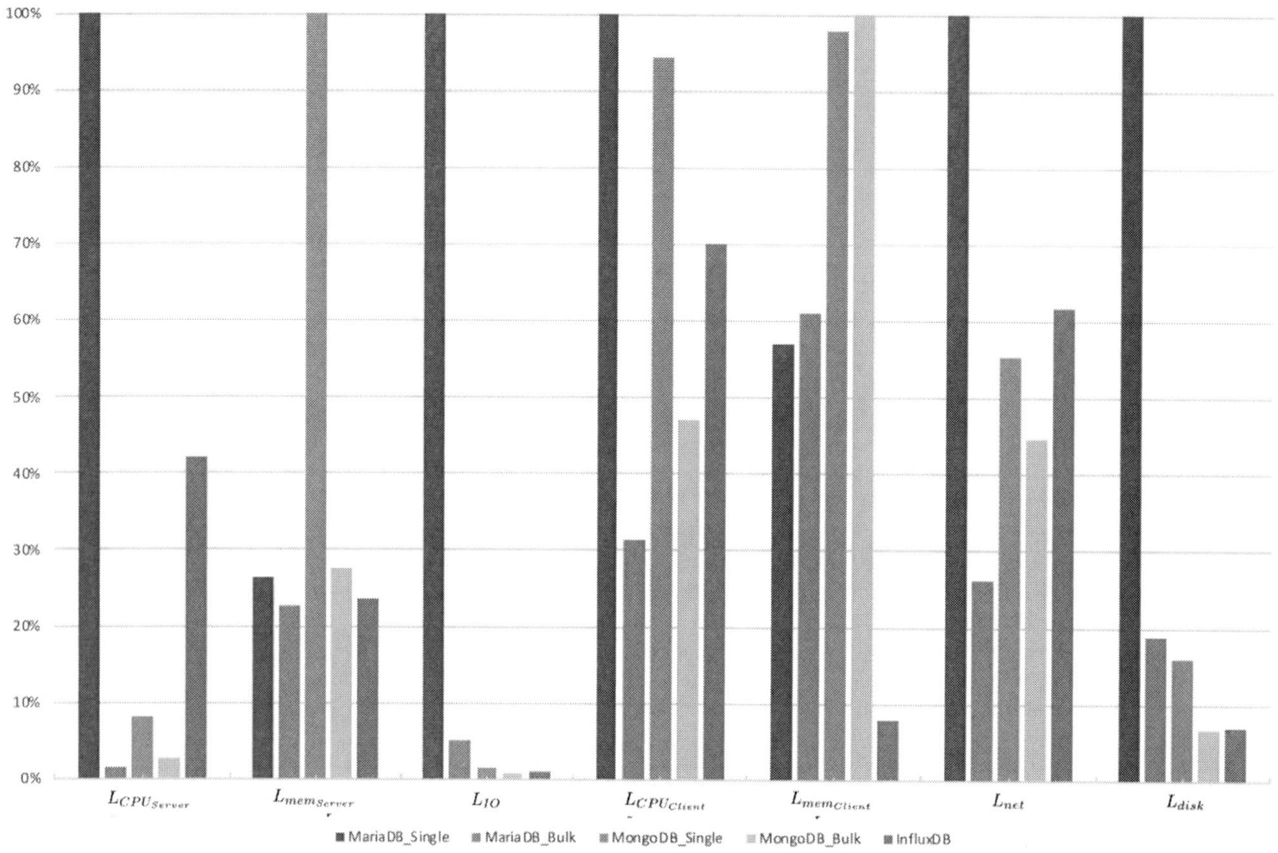

Figure 3. Overview of all Benchmark Values (normalized to respective Maximum)

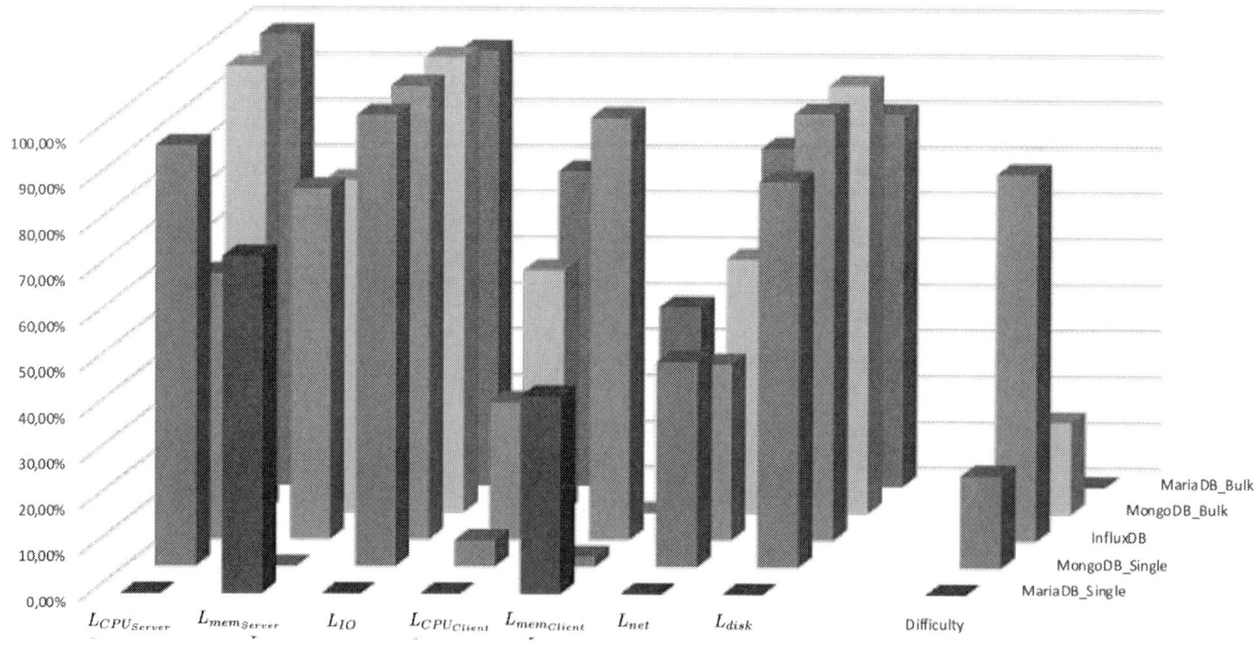

Figure 4. Weighted scores (normalized to maximum score)

Design Method of Wireless Sensor Networks in Railway Environments Considering Power Consumption

Tomoki Kawamura and Nagateru Iwasawa
Telecommunications and Networking Laboratory, Signaling Transport Information Technology Division
Railway Technical Research Institute
Kokubunji-shi, Japan
e-mail: kawamura.tomoki.41@rtri.or.jp

***Abstract*—In recent years, various researches have been conducted for the purpose of applying Wireless Sensor Networks (WSNs) to monitoring the condition of railway facilities. In designing WSNs, it is important to effectively arrange the nodes that compose WSNs. In railway environments, it is necessary to design WSNs in consideration of the presence of obstacles and constraints on the placement. In this paper, we propose a method of calculating an optimal relay nodes placement and a routing method of WSNs in railway environments by combining the mathematical optimization method and Sequential Monte Carlo method.**

Keywords-Wireless sensor network; Optimization method; Power consumption; Sequential Monte Carlo method.

I. INTRODUCTION

Nowadays, with the development of the ICT, researches on the condition monitoring system by mean of a Wireless Sensor Network (WSN) are proceeding. In the railway field as well, various condition monitoring systems by means of WSNs are being researched in order to apply them to such cases as the monitoring of structures along tracks [1], the monitoring of trains [2], and so on [3]. Most of the WSNs consists of sensor nodes for acquiring data of monitored objects, gateways for aggregating data, and relay nodes for transferring data when the sensor nodes and the gateway cannot communicate directly. In designing a WSN, it is important to effectively arrange these nodes. In WSNs for condition monitoring, the locations where sensor nodes and gateways are installed are often predetermined in advance. For this reason, how to efficiently arrange relay nodes is important in designing WSNs, and various researches have been conducted on methods for determining effective placements of relay nodes [4]-[7].

The railway facilities spread long over urban areas and mountainous areas, and there are many obstacles that interrupt wireless communication. In addition, the placement of nodes may be restricted due to safety and physical conditions. Therefore, it is necessary to design WSNs considering these characteristics when introducing WSNs in railway environments.

In this study, we propose a method of calculating an optimal relay nodes placement and the routing of the WSN considering the presence of obstacles and impossible placement in railway environments by combining a mathematical optimization method and Sequential Monte Carlo method.

The rest of the paper is organized as follows. In Section II, we present the related work. Section III presents the envisioned WSN in railway environments. In Section IV, we present the proposed design method of WSN. Section V provides the numerical results of the proposed method. Finally, the paper is concluded in Section IV.

II. RELATED WORK

Research on the relay nodes placement in WSNs is widely conducted and various methods have been proposed such as methods of determining the relay nodes placement so as to maximize the communicable range [4], methods with a focus on fault tolerance [5], methods of determining the efficient relay nodes placement from the viewpoint of network lifetime [6] and methods of determining the placement considering communication cost [7]. However, these methods are targeted at environments without obstacles, and it is assumed that there is no restriction on the node placement. Therefore, these methods are not suitable for environments in which many obstacles exist like railway environments.

In [8], a method for determining the relay nodes placement in consideration of constraints on node placement locations has been proposed. However, even in this method, the presence of obstacles is not taken into consideration, and it is difficult to apply it to railway environments.

Also, in [9], a method of determining the relay nodes placement for the WSN on roads considering the influence of obstacles has been proposed. In this method, the node placement is calculated for the WSN on roads considering the influence of obstacles by using digital maps. Furthermore, in this method, whether or not the intermodal visibility is hindered by obstacles is determined by utilizing the fact that nodes are placed on the road. Therefore, it is difficult to apply this method when nodes are not placed on the road but placed in railway environments.

III. ENVISIONED WSN IN RAILWAY ENVIRONMENTS

In this study, we envision the situation where the WSN consisting of sensor nodes, relay nodes, and a gateway is installed in railway environments. Here, the gateway is a device that gathers data from each sensor node, and the sensor node measures data from monitored objects and transmits the data to the gateway wirelessly. The relay node is a device having a function of relaying sensor data and in cases where data cannot be transmitted from a sensor node directly to a gateway, data is transmitted by multi-hop wireless communication via relay nodes. Additionally, the sensor nodes and the relay nodes are assumed to be driven by batteries. For this reason, it is necessary to replace these batteries before they become empty in order to operate the WSN continuously.

Furthermore, the characteristic of railway environments is that railway facilities spread long over urban areas and mountainous areas, and there are many obstacles that interrupt radio wave propagation. In addition, the placement of nodes may be restricted due to safety and physical conditions in railway environments. In this study, we propose a design method for the WSN to be constructed in railway environments where there are many obstacles and there are constraints on the location of nodes as described above.

IV. PROPOSED DESIGN METHOD OF WSN

In railway environments, it is necessary to monitor a long distance section along railway tracks depending on the objects monitored. Therefore, it is important to construct a WSN in railway environments in such a way that the data can be relayed from each sensor, in which case, as long as each sensor data reaches the gateway, the smaller the number of relay node is, the more economical the WSN is. Also, since the power consumption of each node in the WSN affects battery replacement frequency, the lower the power consumption is, the lower the cost of replacing the batteries.

In this study, we propose a method of calculating the optimal number of relay nodes, the relay node placement and the routing of the WSN considering the presence of obstacles and impossible placement in railway environments by combining a mathematical optimization method and Sequential Monte Carlo method.

The procedure of the method proposed in this paper is shown in Figure 1. In the proposed method, we first optimize the number of relay nodes of the WSN considering the presence of obstacles and places where node placement is impossible in the railway environments. Next, based on the result of the above optimization, we perform the operation simulation of the WSN using time series Monte Carlo method, and calculate the power consumption and data arrival rate of the WSN. Then, we calculate a combination of the optimal relay node placement and the routing method by optimizing from the viewpoint of power consumption of relay nodes based on the power consumption and data arrival rate calculated. The detail of each item in Figure 1 are described below.

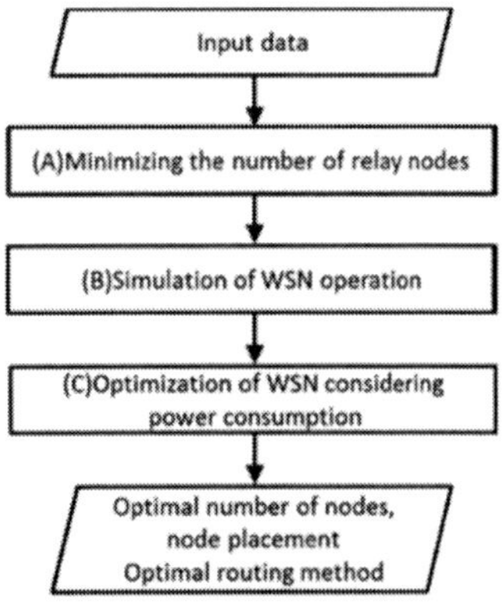

Figure 1. Proposed Design Method of WSN

A. *Minimizing the number of relay nodes*

Regarding minimizing the number of relay nodes, the relay nodes placement in which it is minimized is calculated provided that communication can be established considering the presence of obstacles and places where node placement is impossible in the railway environments. More specifically, the relay nodes placement is calculated by the following optimization setting the minimization of the number of relay nodes as the objective function [10].

[Objective function]

$$\min(R_{num}) \quad (1)$$

[Constraints]

$$r_{i,\mathrm{gat}} = 1 \quad (2)$$

$$P_i(\mathrm{x,y}) \neq N_j(\mathrm{x,y}) \quad (3)$$

In the above equations, R_{num} is the number of relay nodes, and $r_{i,j}$ is the reachability matrix. $r_{i,j}=1$ if there is a route by which data can reach node j from node i, and $r_{i,j}=0$ if there is no reachable route. Also, $P_i(x,y)$ is the position (x coordinate, y coordinate) of the relay node i, and $N_j(x,y)$ is the position (x coordinate, y coordinate) where the relay node cannot be installed. Equation (2) represents the constraint relating to the arrival of data from each sensor node to the gateway, and $r_{i,gat}$ represents the reachability of data from the sensor node i to the gateway. Equation (3) represents the constraint relating to the position of the relay node.

Here, the position $N_j(x,y)$ where the relay node cannot be installed included in the constraint condition is given as input, and it shall be set according to the conditions of the environment where the WSN is installed. In addition, the reachability matrix $r_{i,j}$ is calculated according to the following procedure by giving as input such conditions as the position of the gateway, the number of sensor nodes, the position of each sensor node, the communication distance of each node, and the position of the obstacles.

STEP1 Generation of the adjacency matrix based on the communication distance.

STEP2 Updating the adjacency matrix based on the internodal visibility.

STEP3 Calculation of the reachability matrix based on the adjacency matrix.

Details of the above procedure are shown below.

1) Generation of the adjacency matrix based on the communication distance

In this paper, we consider the reachability matrix showing the reachability of one of the nodes from another by data using the adjacency matrix in the graph theory. The adjacency matrix expresses the presence or absence of the relationship between nodes in the graph, and the adjacency matrix of the graph consisting of n nodes is an n × n square matrix.

Here, on the premise that the adjacency matrix is $a_{i,j}$,

- if there is an edge from node i to node j, $a_{i,j} = 1$.
- if there is no edge from node i to node j, $a_{i,j} = 0$.

In this paper, the gateway, the wireless sensors, and the relays are assumed to be the nodes in the adjacency matrix, and the availability of communication between each node is expressed as an edge. That is, $a_{i,j} = 1$ when communication from node i to node j is possible, and $a_{i,j} = 0$ when communication from node i to node j is impossible.

Here, the determination of whether or not communication is possible between the nodes is made as follows using the communication distance of the wireless devices of the wireless sensor or relay given as the input condition.

- if $D_{i,j} <= C_i$: Communication is possible ($a_{i,j}= 1$),
- if $D_{i,j} > C_i$: Communication is impossible ($a_{i,j} = 0$)

Where, $D_{i,j}$ is the distance between nodes, C_i is the communication distance of each wireless device.

By performing the above judgment between any pair of all the nodes, the adjacency matrix is generated here.

2) *Updating the adjacency matrix based on visibility*

Here, the adjacency matrix generated in STEP1 is updated based on the presence or absence of the internodal visibility. The presence or absence of the internodal visibility is determined based on the position of the obstracles given as input. As shown in Figure 2, the position of the obstacles is input as the coordinates of a line segment constituting the area where the obstacles exist like L_i (x_1, y_1, x_2, y_2). In this paper, the presence or absence of the internodal visibility is judged by the possibility of the intersection of a line segment constituting a certain area of the obstacles and a line segment connecting the nodes. Here, assuming that the two line segments are L_1 (x_1, y_1, x_2, y_2) and L_2 (x_3, y_3, x_4, y_4), the two line segments intersect when the following (4) is satisfied.

$$tc \times td < 0 \tag{4}$$

Where, $tc = (x_1 - x_2)(y_3 - y_1)+(y_1 - y_2)(x_1 - x_3)$,
$td = (x_1 - x_2)(y_4 - y_1)+(y_1 - y_2)(x_1 - x_4)$.

Here, the intersection determination is made based on (4), and if any two of the line segments intersect each other as a result of the judgment, it is determined that there is non-line of sight and the adjacency matrix is updated as $a_{i,j} = 0$ (communication is impossible).

3) *Calculation of the reachability matrix based on the adjacency matrix*

Here, the reachability matrix is calculated based on the adjacency matrix calculated above. The reachability matrix can be calculated by the following procedure.

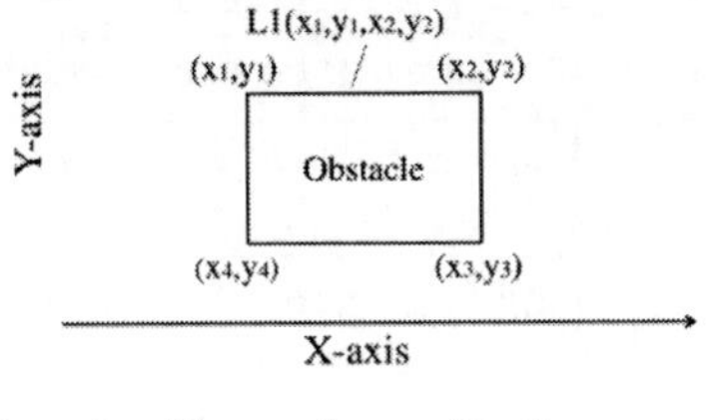

Figure 2. The coordinates of the line segment

STEP1 Add unit matrix I to adjacency matrix A

STEP2 Under the Boolean algebra operation, $A + I$ is repeatedly multiplied by itself r times until the state represented by the following (5) is obtained

$$(A+I)^{r-1} \neq (A+I)^r = (A+I)^{r+1} \tag{5}$$

$(A+I)^{r+1}$ obtained by the above calculation is a reachability matrix. In this way, in the method proposed, the reachability matrix is calculated based on the communication distance of the wireless devices and the line of sight between the nodes.

B. *Simulation of WSN operation*

In simulation of WSN operation, power consumption and data arrival rate of the WSN are calculated based on the number of relay nodes and the arrangement of relay nodes obtained in Section IV-A. At this time, if there are multiple relay nodes placement candidates as a result of the calculation described in Section IV-A, simulation is performed for the plural placement candidates. In this study, we estimate the power consumption and data arrival rate of each node of the WSN in railway environments using sequential Monte Carlo method, which is a method of obtaining approximate solutions by repeatedly performing time series simulation using random numbers. In the proposed method, sequential Monte Carlo method was used to perform simulation considering the routing method, retransmission of data, and communication uncertainty. The configuration of the WSN operation simulation is shown in Figure 3.

The proposed method consists of a WSN evaluation program and routing simulation, and by combining the above two, the power consumption and data arrival rate of sensor nodes and relay nodes are predicted in consideration of the routing methods of the WSN. In the WSN evaluation program, the timing of routing is determined, and the operation of the WSN is simulated based on the result of the routing simulation, and the power consumption and data arrival rate of the WSN are calculated. In the routing simulation, the routing operation is simulated based on the routing method of the WSN to be evaluated, and the routing table is generated. Here, the routing table is a collection of information about routing to the destination contained in each node, and is used to deliver the data. As routing methods used in the WSN, there are a reactive type in which a route is determined immediately before data transmission, a proactive type in which a route is determined in advance before communication, a hybrid type in which both the types are combined, and the like. In railway environments, various monitoring targets exist, but in general, a suitable routing method differs according to the monitoring target. Therefore, when applying the WSN in railway environments, it is important that the design of the WSN includes the routing method. In the proposed method, we estimated the power consumption and data arrival rate of the WSN, including the routing, so that we can examine what kind of routing is desirable.

Next, the flow of the simulation of the WSN is shown in Figure 4. In Figure 4, "time" is the time frame which is being calculated, Δt is the time step width of the simulation. In the simulation of WSN operation, the communication environment at each time frame, and the routing method of the WSN are provided, and the power consumption and the number of communications at each time frame and the data arrival rate of the WSN in railway environments are calculated. To do this, we probabilistically simulated the occurrence of packet loss by a pseudo random number. We ultimately calculated the power consumption and data arrival rate during a stipulated period by repeating the calculations while updating the time frame. Details of each item shown in Figure 4 are discussed below.

1) Input data

In the simulation of WSN operation, the following data are provided as inputs for calculating the power consumption and data arrival rate.

- Routing method of the WSN
- Transmission timing of sensor data
- Number of retransmissions of sensor data
- Position of each node
- Specifications of each node (power consumption, transmission time, etc.)
- Battery capacity
- Communication environment (communicable distance, packet loss rate, etc.) at each position
- Time step width and duration of the simulation

2) Settings of various conditions

In the settings of various conditions, we set the communication environment, and battery health at each time frame in order to calculate the power consumption and data arrival rate at each time frame.

3) Routing simulation

Here, the network is constructed based on the routing method used in the target WSN, and the routing table is generated. In the proposed method, the routing method is simulated by utilizing a network simulator or the like, the routing timing is judged by the WSN evaluation program, and routing simulation is performed when it is judged as the routing timing. The inputs and outputs in the routing simulation are shown below.

[Inputs]

• Position of each node

• Number of retransmissions of data

• Communication environment

[Outputs]

• Number of transmissions and receptions of each node

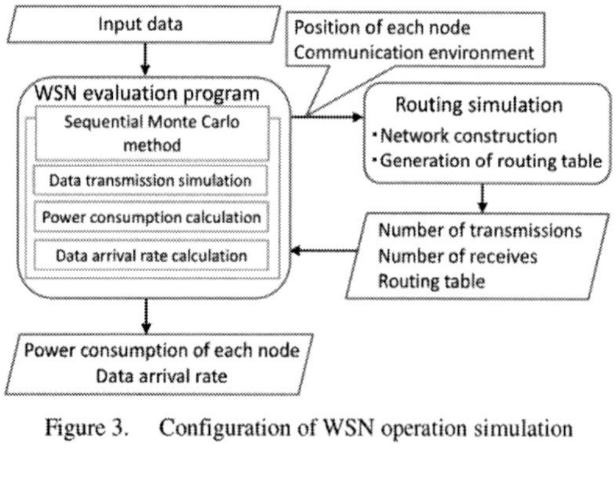

Figure 3. Configuration of WSN operation simulation

• Routing table

4) Simulation of data transmission

Here, we calculate the number of communications of each node and the data arrival rate when data are transmitted from the sensor nodes to the gateway. The calculations are performed on the basis of the conditions set according to various situations. To do this, we probabilistically simulate the occurrence of packet loss by a pseudo random number. Additionally, when packet loss occurs, each node retransmits data until the number of retransmissions reaches the predetermined number of times given as input and calculate the data arrival rate at the gateway and the number of communications (the number of data transmissions and the number of data receptions) of each node in each time frame.

5) Calculation of power consumption in each time frame

Here, we calculate the power consumption of each node in each time frame on the basis of the number of communications calculated in 4). Additionally, the remaining capacity of each sensor node battery is updated on the basis of the calculated power consumption.

In this study, we calculate the power consumption in each time frame using (6) in consideration of the number of transmissions and the number of receptions of each node in each time frame.

$$W_i(t)=P_t \cdot T_t \cdot Nt_i(t)+P_r \cdot T_r \cdot Nr_i(t)+P_w \cdot T_{wi}(t) \quad (6)$$

Here, $W_i(t)$ is the power consumption of sensor node i in time frame t, $Nt_i(t)$ is the number of transmissions of the sensor node i in time frame t, $Nr_i(t)$ is the number of receptions of the sensor node i in time frame t, and $T_{wi}(t)$ is the standby time of the sensor node i in time frame t.

6) Calculation of power consumption and data arrival rate

Here, we calculate the power consumption and data arrival rate during the stipulated period on the basis of the results obtained by repeating the calculations shown in 2) to 5) while updating the time frame. Specifically, we calculate the power consumption of each sensor node up to the stipulated period as the sum value of the power consumption in each time frame. Likewise, we calculate the data arrival rate during the stipulated period of each sensor node on the basis of the sum of the data arrival rates in each time frame.

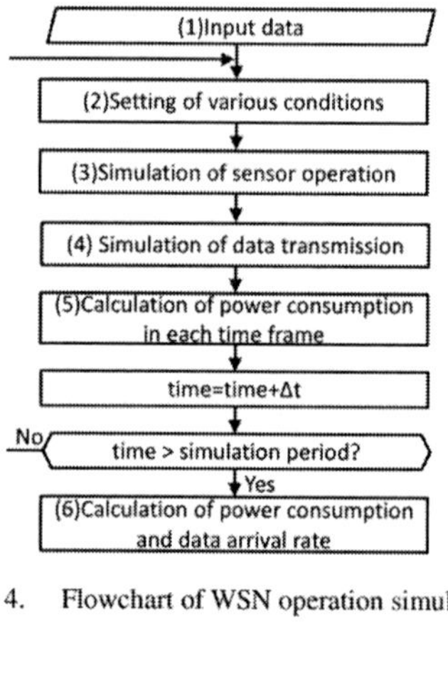

Figure 4. Flowchart of WSN operation simulation

C. Optimization of WSN considering power consumption

In the optimization of WSN considering power consumption, optimization is performed from the viewpoint of the power consumption of the relay node based on the optimum number of relay nodes calculated according to the description in Section IV-A and the node placement candidate, the power consumption of the WSN calculated according to the description in Section IV-B, and the data arrival rate.

The power consumption of the relay node will affect the capacity of the relay node's battery and the network lifetime when operating the WSN. Assuming that the battery capacities of all the relay nodes are the same, the battery of the relay node having the largest power consumption is exhausted first. Therefore, the lifetime of the network depends on the maximum value of the power consumption amount of the relay node. In this study, the WSN was optimized from the viewpoint of the maximization of network lifetime. The objective function can be defined as (7) as the minimization of the maximum value of the power consumption of the sensor node.

[Objective function]

$$\min(\max(W_1,..,W_i)) \tag{7}$$

In the optimization of WSN considering power consumption, it can be formulated as an optimization problem intended for the minimization of the objective function of (7) while satisfying (8) and (9).

[Constraints]

$$A_i \geq A_{\min} \tag{8}$$

$$R_{\text{num}} = R_{num\_min} \tag{9}$$

Where, W_i is the power consumption of node i, A_i is the data arrival rate of node i, $A_{\min}$ is the lower limit value of the data arrival rate, and R_{num_min} is the number of relay nodes obtained by minimizing the number of relay nodes considering railway environments described in Section IV-A. Equation (8) is a constraint on the data arrival rate, and (9) is a constraint on the number of relay nodes and consider limiting the solution to the same number of relay nodes as that obtained in Section IV-A.

Here, $A_{\min}$ included in the constraint condition shall be given as input. For W_i and A_i, the node placement, the routing method, and the number of data retransmissions are given as input, and values are calculated by the simulation of power consumption and data arrival rate described in Section IV-B. In this optimization, the combination of the relay nodes placement, the routing method, and the number of data retransmissions in which, provided that the constraints are satisfied, the objective function is minimized is calculated. This makes it possible to design optimum relay node placement, routing method and the number of date retransmissions from the viewpoint of power consumption.

V. Numerical Experiment

In this section, we performed numerical experiments to verify the usefulness of the proposed method in regard to a WSN installed along a railway line.

A. Calculation condition

We have built a WSN for monitoring a slope condition along a railway line and have carried out demonstration tests [11]. In this study, numerical experiments were carried out for the WSN along the above mentioned railway line. The conditions of the numerical experiments are as follows.

- Figure 5 shows the WSN for monitoring a slope condition in the railway line environment targeted for the numerical experiments. In the targeted WSN, it is assumed that the data is aggregated from two sensors. The monitoring positions of the slope is fixed. In Figure 5, the positions of the sensor nodes are indicated as S, the position of a gateway is indicated as G. Further the positions of places where the nodes cannot be installed are denoted as N, and the positions of the obstacles along the railway line based on the terrain data is denoted by O, and the positions of the. In the numerical experiments, it was studied to select effective relay nodes placement and routing method to make sensor data reach from the sensor nodes to the gateway in the Figure 5. We conducted the numerical experiments under the condition of the communication distance of wireless devices of the sensor nodes and the relay nodes as 170 m with which stable communication can be made in the environment without obstacles according to the measurement result of the wireless device.
- The routing method of WSN is performed by checking the nodes that can communicate by flooding and generating the shortest route. In addition, we examined two patterns of candidates for routing: reconstructing the route every time data is transmitted (reactive type) and reconstructing the route at 0 o'clock every day (proactive type). In addition, the range of 0 to 3 times of data retransmissions was assumed as the candidate.
- The power consumption of the sensor nodes and the relay nodes was assumed to be 69.3 mW when transmitting, 52.8 mW when receieving, and 0.002 mW when standing by, based on the specifications of a commercially available wireless device.
- The transmission cycle of sensor data was set to once per 10 min, and the time step width of the simulation was set to 10 min. Also, it is assumed that power consumption and data arrival rate are calculated as values when WSN is operated for one year.
- The lower limit value of data arrival rate used for the calculation of Section IV-C was set to 95%.

B. Calculation result

Figure 6 shows an example of the result of calculating the relay nodes placement by the proposed method based on the above experiment conditions. As shown in Figure 6, as a result of minimizing the number of relay nodes considering the railway environment, the minimum number of relay nodes was three. In addition, the position indicated by Ri in Figure 6 was obtained as one of the relay node positions which can make all sensor data reach the gateway taking into consideration the obstacles and the positions where the nodes cannot be installed.

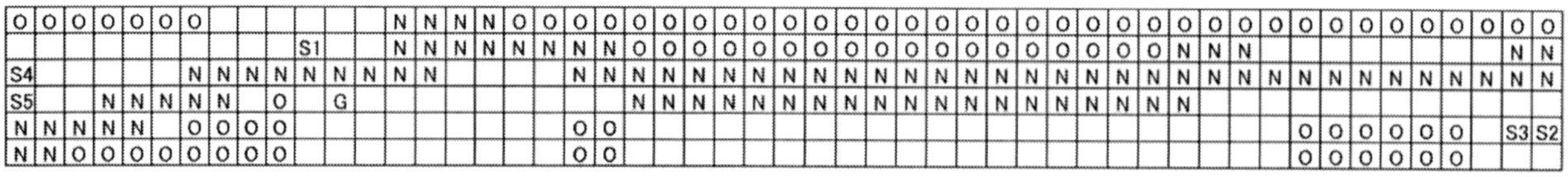

Figure 5. WSN for the numerical experiment (top view of monitoring area)

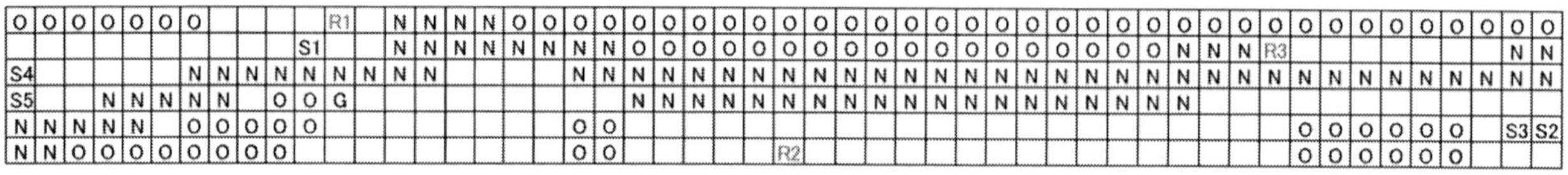

Figure 6. Calculation result of relay nodes placement by the proposed method (top view of monitoring area)

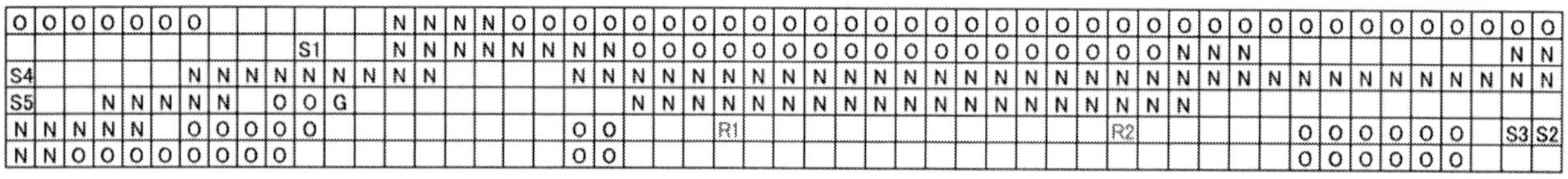

1cell = 10m x 10m, N: the relays installation impossible, O: the obstacles, S: the wireless sensors' location

Figure 6. Calculation result of relay nodes placement by the conventional method (top view of monitoring area)

Next, we optimized the WSN from the viewpoint of power consumption and data arrival rate based on the result of minimizing the number of relay nodes. As a result, it was found out that the optimal solution is setting the routing method to the proactive type and retransmission number to 1 time. Also, the power consumption and data arrival rate of the WSN of the optimal solution are shown in Table I.

Furthermore, for comparison, Table II shows the results in the case where the routing method is different from the conditions in Table I, and Table III shows the results in the case where the number of retransmissions is different from the conditions in Table I. Here, Ret in Table III indicates the number of retransmissions. It can be seen that although the data arrival rate of the two routing methods are not different from each other, the reactive type has higher power consumption from Table II. This is probably because the frequency of the reactive type routing is larger than that of the proactive type under the set condition, and the power consumption by routing is increased.

TABLE I. SIMULATION RESULT OF OPTIMUL WSN

	S1	S2	S3	S4	S5	R1	R2	R3
Power consumption (Wh)	1.13	1.12	1.12	1.13	1.13	5.56	3.77	3.77
Data arrival rate (%)	99.7	97.8	97.7	99.8	99.3	-	-	-

TABLE II. SIMULATION RESULT OF REACTIVE ROUTING

	S1	S2	S3	S4	S5	R1	R2	R3
Power consumption (Wh)	10.2	9.16	9.16	10.2	10.2	24.7	22.9	19.8
Data arrival rate (%)	99.7	97.8	97.7	99.8	99.3	-	-	-

Next, regarding the number of retransmissions, it can be seen from Table III that increasing the number of retransmissions increases the data arrival rate and also increases the power consumption. Since the data arrival rate is set to 95% as the condition of the optimization this time, it is considered that one time, the minimum number of retransmissions was selected within the range that satisfies this condition.

Finally, we compare the conventional method for determining the relay nodes placement that does not consider the influence of obstacles with the proposed method. Here, we calculated the relay nodes placement by a method not considering the influence of obstacles by calculating the determination of the relay nodes placement that minimizes the number of relay nodes in Section IV-A without considering the influence of obstacles. Figure 6 shows the result of determining the relay nodes placement by a method not considering the influence of obstacles. In Figure 6, the number of relay nodes is two, and it is smaller than the result by the proposed method. However, with the placement of the relay nodes in Figure 6, data from S2, S3, S5 cannot reach the gateway due to the influence of the obstacles.

TABLE III. SIMULATION RESULT OF DIFFERENT RETRANSMISSIONS

		S1	S2	S3	S4	S5	R1	R2	R3
Ret=0	Power consumption (Wh)	1.08	1.07	1.07	1.08	1.08	4.89	3.35	3.50
	Data arrival rate (%)	95.0	81.5	81.5	95.0	90.3	-	-	-
Ret=2	Power consumption (Wh)	1.13	1.13	1.13	1.13	1.13	5.64	3.80	3.79
	Data arrival rate (%)	99.9	99.8	99.8	99.9	99.9	-	-	-
Ret=3	Power consumption (Wh)	1.13	1.13	1.13	1.13	1.13	5.64	3.81	3.79
	Data arrival rate (%)	99.9	99.9	99.9	99.9	99.9	-	-	-

It is considered that in this way, the number of relay nodes, the nodes placement, and the routing method can be designed considering the influence of the obstacles in railway environments on the radio communication by using the proposed method.

VI. CONCLUSION

In this paper, we proposed a method to calculate the optimal relay nodes placement and routing of the WSN considering the presence of the obstacles and the positions impossible for installment in railway environments by combining a mathematical optimization method and Sequential Monte Carlo method. Additionally, we demonstrated the usefulness of the proposed method by performing numerical experiments using the proposed method for WSN installed along a railway line.

In the future, we plan to proceed with the verification of the proposed method, and consider effective nodes placement and routing method of WSN in railway environments under various conditions using the proposed method.

REFERENCES

[1] R. Bischoff, J. Meyer, O. Enochsson, G. Feltrin, and L. Elfgren, "Eventbased strain monitoring on a railway bridge with a wireless sensor network," in Proc. 4th Int. Conf. Struct. Health Monitor. Intell. Infrastructure, Zurich, pp. 1-8, 2009.

[2] A. L. Schiavo, "Fully Autonomous Wireless Sensor Network for Freight Wagon Monitoring," IEEE Sensors Journal, vol. 16, no. 24, pp. 9053-9063, 2016.

[3] V. J. Hodge, S. O'Keefe, M. Weeks, and A. Moulds, "Wireless Sensor Networks for Condition Monitoring in the Railway Industry: A Survey," IEEE Trans. Intell Transp., vol. 16, no. 3, pp. 1088-1106, 2015.

[4] W. Guo, X. Huang, W. Lou, and C. Liang,"On relay node placement and assignment for twotiered wireless networks," Mobile Networks and Applications, vol.13, no.1-2, pp.186-197, 2008.

[5] D. Yang, S. Misra, X. Fang, G. Xue, and J. Zhang, "Two-tiered constrained relay node placement in wireless sensor networks:Computational complexity and efficient approximations," IEEE Trans. Mob Comput., vol. 11, no. 8, pp. 1399-1411, 2012.

[6] X. Cheng, D. Du, L. Wang, and B. Xu, "Relay sensor placement in wireless sensor networks," ACM/Springer Wireless Netw., vol. 14,no. 3, pp. 425-443, 2007.

[7] M. Nikolov, and Z.J. Haas, "Relay Placement in Wireless Networks: Minimizing Communication Cost," IEEE Trans. Wireless Commun., vol. 15, no. 5, pp. 3587-3602, 2016.

[8] M. Bagaa, A. Chelli, D. Djenouri, and T. Taleb, "Optimal Placement of Relay Nodes Over Limited Positions in Wireless Sensor Networks," IEEE Trans. Wireless Commun., vol. 16, no. 4, pp. 2205-2219, 2017.

[9] H. Imai, K. Mase, H. Okada, and K. Nakano, "Relay Node Placement of Wireless Multi-hop Networks Using Line-of-Sight Spaces over Road Surface", IEICE Trans. B, Vol.J99-B, no.10, pp.871-880, 2016. (in Japanese)

[10] N. Iwasawa, T. Kawamura, M. Nozue, S. Ryuo, and N. Iwaki, "Design of Wireless Sensor Network in the Railway", 7th International Conference on Sensor Networks, pp.122-127, 2018.

[11] M. Nozue et al.," Wi-SUN Monitoring System for Railway Facilities", IEICE Technical Report, vol.117, no.352, pp. 41-46, 2017.

Routing Algorithm Based on the Transmission History for Monitoring Railway Vehicles

Nagateru Iwasawa, Satoko Ryuo, Tomoki Kawamura and Nariya Iwaki
Signalling and Transport Information Technology Division
Railway Technical Research Institute
Tokyo, Japan
e-mail: iwasawa.nagateru.81@rtri.or.jp

Abstract— **Efforts have been made to utilize the Wireless Sensor Network (WSN) to monitor the state of railway facilities, such as structures, tracks, vehicles, etc. In monitoring the condition of railway cars, items such as the brakes, the train speed, the truck vibration, etc. are subjected to monitoring. We are developing a system under which the crew can monitor the condition of the train's vehicle in real time. In cases where data are transmitted when the train is running, it is assumed that the communication distance between the wireless terminals changes according to changes in the radio wave propagation environment. Therefore, in this paper, we propose a transmission method when the train is driving, and also conduct a functional verification test by an actual machine.**

Keywords*-*routing algorithm; railway vehicle; monitoring; radio wave environment.

I. INTRODUCTION

Recently, with the development of information and communication technology, studies on the monitoring of the condition of the railway facilities by using the WSN have been in progress [1][2]. They cover diverse fields, such as the structures, the tracks, the overhead contact lines and the vehicles. Furthermore, the purpose of the monitoring is extensive. Two examples are the detection of abnormal values due to sudden condition changes, such as the landslide and derailment, and understanding, via long-term monitoring, of the tendency to deterioration of the facilities. In the railway vehicle condition monitoring, data such as the control information of brakes and air conditioning, train speed, train positions, temperature and vibration of the bogie are collected. In this paper, our purpose of the railway vehicle monitoring is that the crew of the train confirms the control information of the brake in a minute.

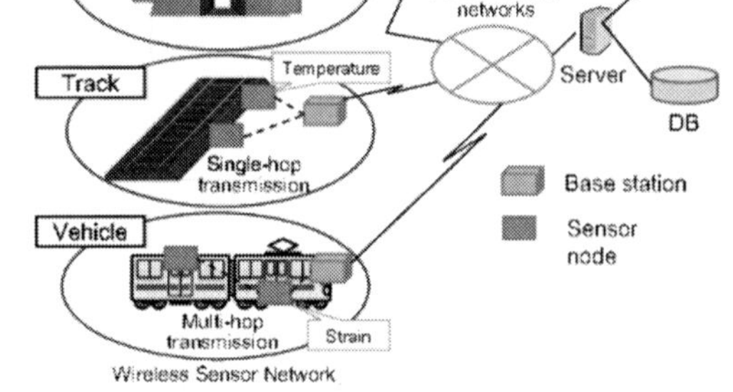

Figure 1. Example of WSN for railway condition monitoring

Figure 1 shows a typical WSN setup for railway condition monitoring [2]. The WSN consists of sensor nodes that measure the physical quantity and wirelessly transmit it as sensor data and a base station that collects data. Furthermore, the base station transmits the data to the server via a network like the mobile telephone network as necessary. Also, the server accumulates the data in the Data Base (DB). The users can access the data in the DB via the public or the private network. In the train consisting of multiple vehicles, if the vehicles condition is monitored, the sensor nodes of the WSN are installed linearly. The ways of the transmission the sensor data from these sensors to the base station are single-hop and multi-hop. Besides, in areas where fixed power sources, such as a bogie cannot be supplied, the sensor nodes are driven by the batteries, so efficient power consumption is required. When the distance between the lead vehicle and the last vehicle is several hundred meters, in order to make a single-hop network, it is necessary to increase the transmission power. Of course, there is a possibility that direct communication between the lead vehicle's node and the last vehicle's node cannot be performed with the prescribed transmission power. So, it is important that the WSN of the train need efficient multi-hop routing. For example, some sensor nodes are grouped, and one sensor node in each group aggregates the sensor data, and the base station collects data via the aggregated sensor nodes [3][4][5]. In addition, a method of constructing a Wireless Personal Area Network (WPAN) using ZigBee for communication within a group and configuring a Wireless Local Network (WLAN) using Wi-Fi for communication between groups and base stations has been proposed [6]. However, the sensor nodes included in each group are fixed, so it is not taken into consideration that the coupling given thought that the coupling and the decoupling train vehicles causes groups and the base station to change. And the wireless communication technology for WSN called Low Power Wide Area (LPWA), such as LoRaWAN and SIGFOX can be construct a fixed wide network. So, it is applicable as long as the train set does not change.

On the other hand, in the ad hoc network, it is possible to construct a network with a base station and the sensor nodes among neighbor vehicles and collect data. So, it is suitable for a system under which all the sensor data of the trains in the area are accumulated in the DB and the users can browse the data in it. But in such a system, overhead occurs when the train crew browse the data in the DB due to data transmission from the base station to the DB and the access to the data by the train crew. Therefore, it is necessary to construct a network among the base station and the sensor nodes of one train set so as to reduce the length of time until the crew checks the data. For example, it is possible to construct an ad hoc network between the base station and the sensor nodes by manually setting the same network IDentification (ID) on base station and sensor nodes. But considering the time required for setting the network ID and the possibility of misconfiguration, it is desirable to automatically construct the network in the train set. In ad hoc network research, a method of estimating the location of a sensor node based on the Received Signal Strength Indicator (RSSI), the Time Of Arrival (TOA) and the Time Difference Of Arrival (TDOA) has been proposed [7]. However, it is not realistic because it may result in errors with a probability of 50% or more. Also, instead of the Global Positioning System (GPS) with high power consumption, a method capable of discriminating between vehicles of the same train and different train based on the correlation between the data for several seconds obtained from the acceleration sensor has been proposed [8]. However, there are problems in that it is necessary to scale down in order to implement it on the Central Processing Unit (CPU) of the sensor node, etc., because MATrix LABoratory (MatLab) [9] analyzes data offline.

Therefore, we have proposed a system configuration and a method of automatically constructing a closed network within a train set at the time of the train is stopping at a station, taking into consideration the coupling and decoupling [10]. In this paper, we propose a method of efficiently collecting data in the network of the system mentioned above at the time the train is running.

The rest of the present paper is organized as follows: Section II presents our proposed system for the railway vehicle monitoring. In Section III, we propose the routing algorithm for the monitoring system at the time the train is running. In Section IV, we implement the proposed algorithm in a prototype, and we indicate the result of the function verification test with it in Section V. Finally, Section VI concludes the present paper.

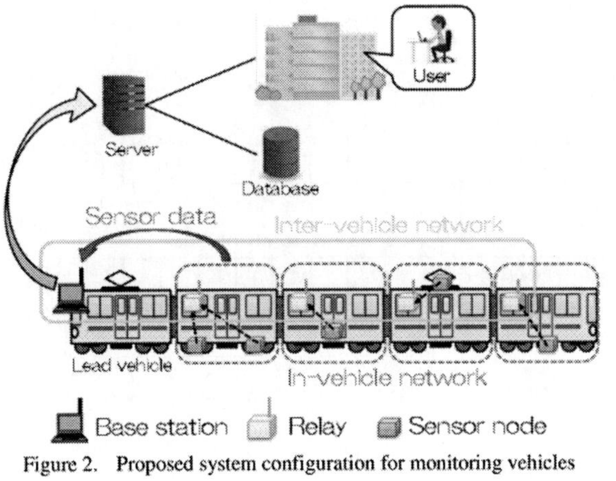

Figure 2. Proposed system configuration for monitoring vehicles

II. SYSTEM PROPOSED

A. *System Configuration [10]*

Figure 2 shows the system configuration we have proposed regarding the construction of a network for each train set for collecting data. First, the in-vehicle network consists of a relay and sensor nodes in one vehicle. The relay relays the sensor data from the sensor nodes. The networking components of this network are not variable even if the train set changes according to the coupling and decoupling, so it may be a fixed network. Therefore, the communication between the relay and the sensor node in this network is possible using a wired as well as a wireless network.

Next, the inter-vehicle network consists of a base station and relays in one train set. The base station collects the sensor data from the relays. The base station comprehends the vehicles and the relays of its own train and constructs a network based on the organization information in the operation plan of the vehicles. By selecting a frequency band different from that of the in-vehicle network, it is possible to communicate using the in-vehicle network independently from the communication which is being made simultaneously using the in-vehicle network, suppressing the interference in the own system.

B. *Problem of Communication at the Time the Train is Runnning*

There is concern that the communication quality at the time the train is running fluctuates under the fading and the influence of change in radio environment. Figure 3 shows the measurement results of the radio environment of a band of 920MHz, which is the Industrial, Scientific and Medical (ISM) band of Japan at two stations in the suburban and urban areas. Figure 4 shows a scene of the measurement. It indicates that the frequency used differs according to the location. Therefore, when using a specific frequency, it is assumed that the communication quality fluctuates as the location changes. In particular, it is thought that the influence on long-range inter-vehicle communication is greater than the in-vehicle communication. In this paper, we propose a routing algorithm in the inter-vehicle network considering change in communication environment.

III. PROPOSAL OF NEW ROUTING ALGORITHM

A. *Transmission Matrix[10]*

In the inter-vehicle network of the system proposed, a transmission matrix as show in the Table I is created at the time of network configuration and it is memorized in the base station. Since the transmission matrix is created based on the train sets information and communication confirmation, the physical distance and the communication environment at the time of network configuration are taken into consideration. The relay number represents a vehicle number, for example, relay 1 means a relay of the first vehicle. The vehicle number is a unique number of a vehicle, and the same number does not exist elsewhere. And 1 in the Table I indicates a communication candidate link, 0 indicates that it is not a communication candidate link. For example, between the base station and relay 1, 2, 3 there are communication candidate links. It means that the communication candidates of the base station are relay 1, 2 and 3. In addition, we assume symmetric communication quality, the communication candidate of relay 1, 2 and 3 is the base station. Also, if the communication toward the base station is designated as the communication in the uplink direction and the communication toward the relay as the communication in the downlink direction, the base station and the relays hold uplink direction and downlink direction communication candidates in the routing table respectively. For example, relay 2 holds {Base station, Relay 1} as the uplink communication candidate, {Relay 3, Relay 4} as the downlink communication candidate in the routing table. In the data collection immediately after the network configuration in stopped train, based on this routing table, the routing is performed with the number of hops as a metric in [10]. When changes in the communication environment are not considered, it is desirable to transfer data to the relay close to the destination node and reduce the total number of hops, thereby reducing the total power consumption in the

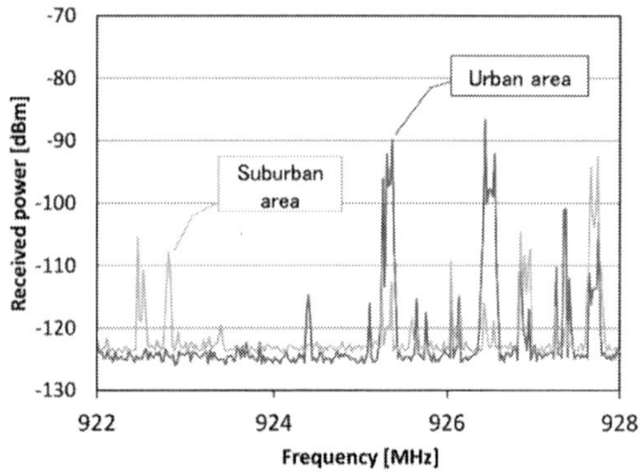

Figure 3. Measurement results of radio environment

Figure 4. Scenery of measuring radio environment

network. However, if the communication quality deteriorates and data cannot be transferred from the relay 3 to the base station, the relay 3 tries to transfer them to the relay 1. Changing the transfer destination causes an increase in the power consumption due to retrial and in the latency due to timeout.

B. Routing Algorithm Considering Environmental Change

As a method of grasping changes in the communication environment, there is a method of periodically sending the hello packets between nodes as communication candidates and monitoring the RSSI [6]. However, periodic packet transmission increases the traffic of the entire network, and the power consumption of the entire network also increases. Therefore, we examined a method of dynamically determining a transfer destination from communication candidates based on the result of past data communication. Regardless of the frequency of hello packets, it does not need the power to transmit them. The base station and the relays hold a table of an arbitrary length $\alpha + 1$ called a transmission history table; one for the uplink direction (called forward history table) and the other for the downlink direction (called backward history table). Figure 5 shows an example of the transmission history table of relay2 in Table I. They hold the result of, in order of lateness, the most recent to the αth transmissions which were made in the uplink direction and those in the downlink direction and the downlink direction and update them in the First In First Out (FIFO) format. Character 1 in the transmission history table indicates successful data transmission and character 0 in it indicates data transmission failure. The data transmission failure or success is judged by the presence of the ACKnowledgement (ACK) from the destination node to the source node. The first column always holds 1. If it does not hold 1, there is a

TABLE I. EXAMPLE OF TRANSMISSION MATRIX

	Relay 1	Relay 2	Relay 3	Relay 4	Relay 5
Base station	1	1	1	0	0
Relay 1	—	1	1	0	0
Relay 2	—	—	1	1	0
Relay 3	—	—	—	1	1
Relay 4	—	—	—	—	1

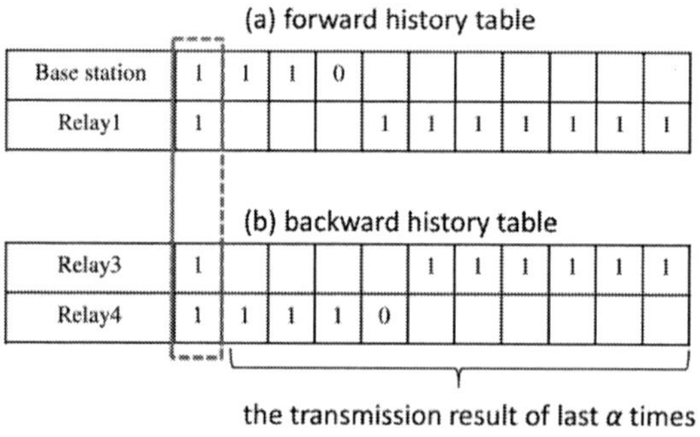

Figure 5. Example of a transmission history table

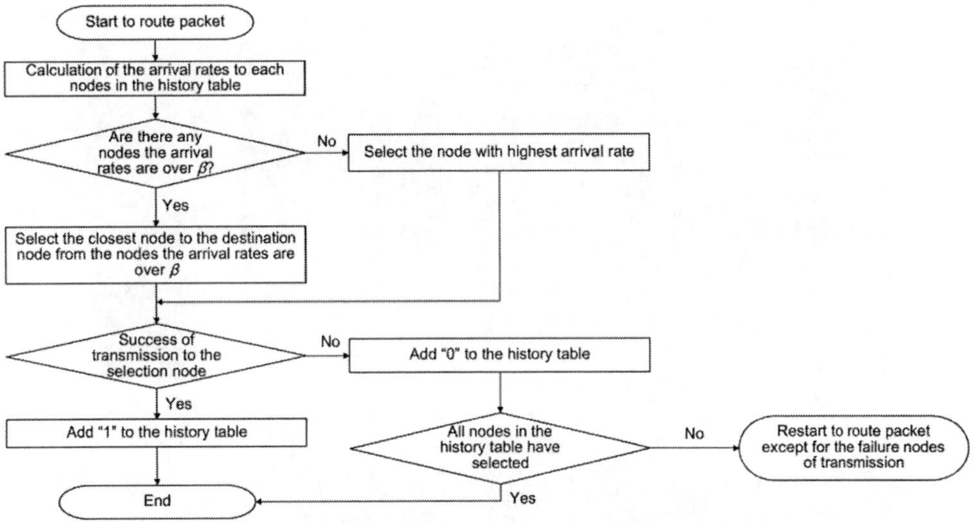

Figure 6. Basic procedure for determining the transfer destination relay

Base station	1	1	1	0								75%
Relay1	1				1	1	1	1	1	1	1	100%

↓

Base station	1	1	0									67%
Relay1	1			1	1	1	1	1	1	1	1	100%

↓

Base station	1	0										50%
Relay1	1		1	1	1	1	1	1	1	1	1	100%

↓

Base station	1											100%
Relay1	1	1	1	1	1	1	1	1	1	1	1	100%

Figure 7. Example of the operation of the transmission procedure

possibility that the node whose priority has dropped due to deterioration of the radio wave environment may not be selected again. This leads to the increase in the number of hops. Therefore, holding 1 in this column, it is possible to raise the priority again for the node whose priority has dropped.

Figure 6 shows the basic procedure for determining the transfer destination relay based on the transmission history table. The arrival rate is the probability that a transmission from a node to the other node in a specific period $\alpha + 1$ has succeeded. This algorithm preferentially selects the furthest node among the nodes whose arrival rate is higher than the threshold value β set. In the forward history table of relay 2 in fig. 5 (a), we will assume β, which is the threshold of arrival rate, to be 0.9. Figure 7 shows an example of the operation of the transmission procedure. First, in fig. 5 (a), since the rate of arrival at the base station is 0.75 and the rate of arrival at relay 1 is 1.0, transmission from relay 2 to relay 1 the arrival rate of which is greater than β in the uplink direction is selected. After that, the forward history table in cases where it was transferred to relay 1 successfully is shown in fig. 7. Next, the table is updated with the passage of time, and the arrival rate from relay 2 to the base station decreases. Last, since the rate of arrival from relay 2 at the base station and that at relay 1 are both 1, base station is selected in the next transmission. In this way, by always holding 1 in the first column, the relay which failed in transmission is also selected again. Therefore, when the communication environment is improved, it can be expected to reduce the number of hops. It is assumed that the communication distance between nodes changes according to changes in the radio wave propagation environment. However, even if this algorithm is used in the environment where the communication distance does not change, the performance equivalent to the hop metric algorithm.

TABLE II. SPECIFICATIONS OF THE WIRELESS MODULE

Standards-compliant	ARIB STD-T108 (Japan), IEEE 802.15.4g/e
Frequency	922.3 ~ 928.1 MHz
Band width	200 kHz, 400 kHz
Modulation method	2GFSK
Baud rate	50 kbps, 100 kbps
Transmission power	1 mW, 10 mW, 20 mW

IV. IMPLEMENTATION

We implemented the proposed method described in Section III(B) in a prototype. Figure 8 shows the prototype. The base station consists of a wireless module and a laptop that controls it. And the relay consists of a wireless module, a CPU board that controls it, and a battery. Table II shows the specifications of the wireless module [11]. Then, Figure 9 shows the frame format in the inter-vehicle network. In this

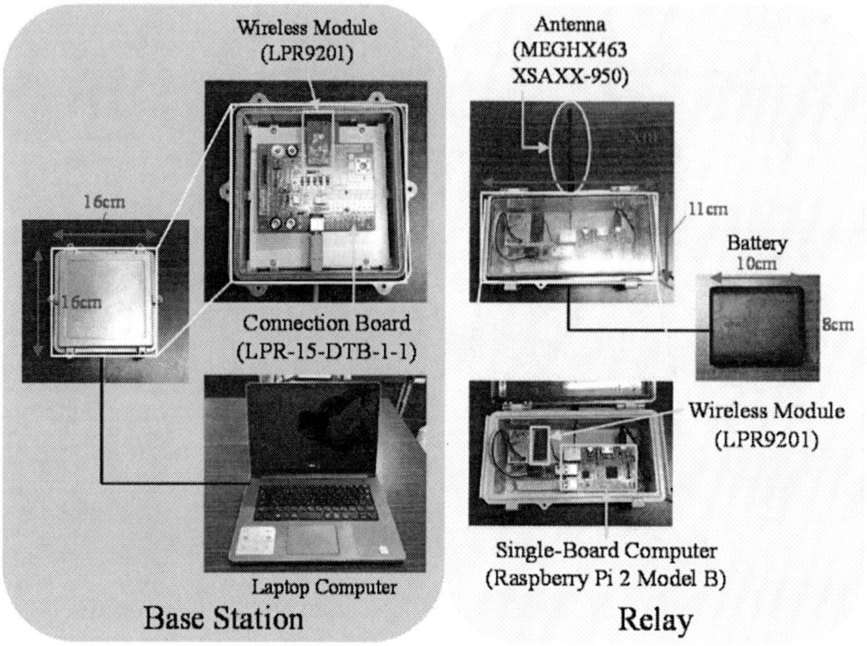

Figure 8. Prototype of the base station and the relay

Max 500 bytes

Sequence frame number [4 bytes]	Frame control [1 byte]	Reserved [2 bytes]	Retry number [1 byte]	Source node ID [5 bytes]	Destination node ID [5 bytes]	Payload [variable]	Frame check sequence [2 bytes]

Figure 9. Frame format of the prototype in the inter-vehicle network

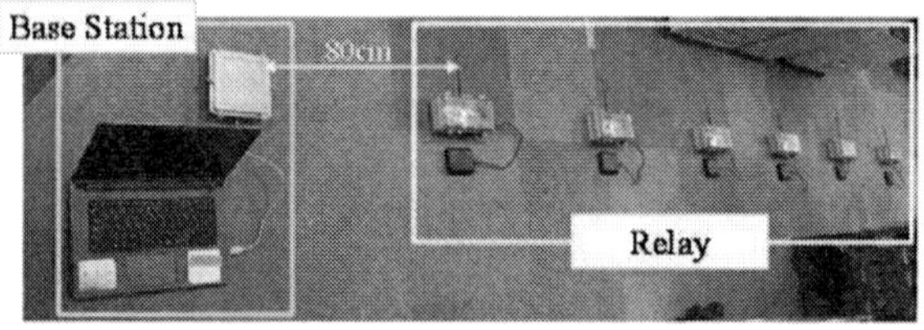

Figure 10. Scenery of the experiment

paper, we set 8 bytes of dummy data for the payload assuming 1 byte of data length, 4 bytes of dates and time, and 3 bytes of sensor data.

The data collection sequence of this prototype is that the base station sequentially performs data request and data reception for each relay. Therefore, by reconsidering the data collection sequence, the processing time can be expected to reduce.

V. Experiment

We conducted an experiment to confirm the function of data transmission taking account of the changes in the radio wave environment using the prototype introduced in Section IV. Figure 10 shows the scenery of the experiment. Inside the room, one base station and ten relays were linearly arranged at 80-cm intervals. Also, the transmission power was 1 mW. For this experiment, the sensor data are collected from all relays once. After collecting data 5 times, the antennas were removed and data were collected again 5 times. After that, the antennas were attached and data were collected 5 times. We simulated the radio environmental change by detaching and attaching the antennas. These operations were carried out by the method which was applied with the number of hops as a metric, and they were repeated by the method proposed, and then evaluation was made based on the length of time required for data collection. In the proposed method, we assumed that the length of the table $\alpha = 3$ and the threshold of the arrival rate $\beta = 0.9$. Since this is a function verification test, α was set to be small and β was set to a large value in order to frequently change the node selection. Table III shows the experimental results. The values in Table III represent the average time. The average length of time required for data collection of the first five and the last five operations conducted with the antennas attached is about 36 seconds. On the other hand, that of the intermediate five operations conducted with the antennas detached is 103.7 seconds, almost 3 times as long as 36 seconds, when the former method is applied, and 48.9 seconds, 1.4 times as long as 36 seconds, when the latter method (the method proposed) is applied. In this

TABLE III. RESULT OF THE EXPERIMENT (AVERAGE TIME)

	First 5 times (antenna attached) [s]	Next 5 times (antenna detached) [s]	Last 5 times (antenna attached) [s]
Hop number metric	36.1	103.7	37.6
Proposed method	35.8	48.9	36.1

environmental condition change, the difference in length of time required for data collection between the two methods becomes about two times. If we apply the method proposed, the communication distance is actually shortened, and we confirmed that in the static environment, under the method proposed the node which sends data is capable of switching the forwarding destination to the node closer to it, and that the method proposed is effective when change in radio wave propagation environment occurs.

VI. CONCLUSION AND FUTURE WORK

We are developing a monitoring system aimed at confirming control information, such as brakes in real time in crew members. We have been transmitting hop count metrics for stoppage until now. In this paper, we propose a data transmission method considering radio wave environment change during driving. We implemented the proposed method in prototype and carried out function verification test. We simulated the deterioration of the radio wave environment and the time required for data collection became less than half, so we confirmed that it is effective when the radio wave environment deteriorates. In addition, it was confirmed that even when the environment improved, it returned to the state before deterioration. In the future we will study the following.

- How to set the appropriate length and threshold of the transmission history table

If the length of the transmission history table α is short and the threshold value β is high, steep change can be made, the length of that α is long and it can deal with gentle fluctuation if the threshold value β is low. It is necessary to appropriately set them according to the allowable delay of data and the acquisition interval.

- Method of leveling power consumption

In the proposed method, since the communication time becomes shorter, it can be expected that the electric load of the whole network is reduced. However, even if a specific relay is loaded, it will not be avoided. Considering battery replacement, it is also important that no load is placed on a specific relay.

- Demonstration experiment of running condition

Since the experiment in this paper was carried out in a stationary state, it is important to demonstrate even in the running state.

REFERENCES

[1] G. M. Shafiullah, A. Gyasi-Agyei, and P. Wolfs, "Survey of Wireless Communications Applications in the Railway Industry," The 2nd international conference on Wireless Broadband and Ultra Wideband Communications (AusWireless 2007), Aug. 2007, pp.65-70, doi: 10.1109/AUSWIRELESS.2007.74.

[2] V. J. Hodge, S. O'Keefe, M. Weeks, and A. Moulds, "Wireless Sensor Networks for Condition Monitoring in the Railway Industry: A Survey," IEEE Transactions on Intelligent Transportation Systems, Nov. 2014, pp. 1088-1106, doi: 10.1109/TITS.2014.2366512.

[3] H. Scholten, R. Westenberg, and M. Schoemaker, "Trainspotting, a WSN-based train integrity system," Proceedings of ICN 2009, March 2009, Gosier, France, pp. 226-231, IEEE Computer Society Presse, DOI: 10.1109/ICN.2009.59.

[4] N. Wang, Y. Liang, and L. Wang, "On-line Monitoring Method of Bearing in Rotating Machinery Based on Wireless Sensor Networks," The 3rd international forum on energy, environment science and materials (IFEESM 2017), Jan. 2017, pp. 564-571, doi: 10.2991/ifeesm-17.2018.107.

[5] W. Nan, M. Qingfeng, Z. Bin, L. Tong, and M. Qinghai, "Research on Linear Wireless Sensor Networks Used for Online Monitoring of Rolling Bearing in Freight Train," Journal of Physics: Conference Series, vol.305, no. 1, July 2011, pp. 1-10 doi: 10.1088/1742-6596/305/1/012024.

[6] P. Mahasukhon, et al., "A study on energy efficient multi-tier multi-hop wireless sensor networks for freight-train monitoring," The 7th international wireless communications and mobile computing conference (IWCMC), Aug. 2011, pp. 297-301, doi: 10.1109/IWCMC.2011.5982549.

[7] A. Savvides, C. Han, and M. B. Strivastava, "Dynamic Fine-Grained Localization in Ad-Hoc Networks of Sensors," The 7th annual international conference on Mobile computing and networiking (Mobicom '01), 2001, pp. 166-179, doi: 10.1145/381677.381693.

[8] H. Scholten, R. Westenberg and M. Schoemaker, "Sensing Train Integrity," the IEEE International Conference on Sensors, Oct. 2009, pp. 669-674, doi: 10.1109/ICSENS.2009.5398340.

[9] MathWorks, https://mathworks.com/ [retrieved: August 2018]

[10] S. Ryuo, N. Iwasawa, T. Kawamura, A. Hada, and K. Kawasaki, "Method for Creating Networks between Vehicles to Monitor Vehicle Condition," Quarterly Report of RTRI, vol. 58, no. 4, pp. 285-291, Nov. 2017, doi: https://doi.org/10.2219/rtriqr.58.4_285.

[11] SATORI ELECTRIC CO., LTD., http://www.satori.co.jp/english/ [retrieved: August 2018]

Behavior Modeling of Networked Wireless Sensors for Energy Consumption Using Petri Nets

Jin-Shyan Lee
Department of Electrical Engineering
National Taipei University of Technology (Taipei Tech.)
Taipei, Taiwan
e-mail: jslee@mail.ntut.edu.tw

Yuan-Heng Sun
Information & Communications Research Labs
Industrial Technology Research Institute (ITRI)
Hsinchu, Taiwan
e-mail: gilbertsun@itri.org.tw

Abstract— **Energy efficiency is a critical design issue in wireless sensor networks. In order to analyze the energy consumption of a single node, a system model of networked wireless sensors is thus required. Based on a Petri net framework, this paper is proposing a systematic approach to the modeling and measurement of energy consumption for ZigBee-equipped sensors. Moreover, an experiment has been conducted to measure the real power consumption and to provide input parameters to the Petri net model. The comparative results show that the Petri net model could approximate the real measurement under the assumed scenarios. It is believed that the technique presented in this paper could be further applied to complex and non-periodic operations in wireless sensor networks.**

Keywords-energy consumption; Petri nets; sensor models; wireless sensor networks; ZigBee.

I. INTRODUCTION

Recently, there has been an increasing emphasis on developing distributed Wireless Sensor Networks (WSNs) with self-organization capabilities to cope with device failures, changing environmental conditions, and different sensing and measurement applications [1]-[4]. WSNs consist of hundreds or even thousands of networked wireless sensors which are linked by radio frequencies to perform distributed sensing tasks. In general, since these wireless sensors are equipped with batteries, energy consumption is a major design issue. Researchers have attempted to determine the best topology, the optimal way of routing, or whether the sensor node should aggregate data or not. All these topics are investigated with the intention of prolonging network lifetime from a global networking point of view [5]-[7].

On the other hand, from a single node point of view, the energy conservation could be achieved by applying some power management techniques. However, in order to propose methods by which power consumption can be minimized in networked wireless sensors, it is first necessary to gain an accurate understanding of their energy consumption characteristics. Thus, a system model of wireless sensors is required so as to analyze the energy consumption of a single node.

Starting from measurements carried out on the off-the-shelf radio, Bougard *et al.* [8] evaluated the potential of an IEEE 802.15.4 radio for use in an ultra-low power sensor node operating in a dense network. Their resulting model has been used to optimize the parameters of both the physical and medium access control layers in a dense sensor network scenario. Also, based on the empirical energy consumption measurements of Bluetooth modules, Ekstrom *et al.* [9] presented a realistic model of the radio energy consumption for Bluetooth-equipped sensor nodes used in a low-duty-cycle network. Their model gives users the possibility to optimize their radio communication with respect to energy consumption while sustaining the data rate. From a hybrid system point of view, Sousa *et al.* [10] modeled and analyzed the power consumption of a wireless sensor node in sensor networks using differential hybrid Petri Nets (PNs). With the discrete event evolution, the continuous battery discharge profile is updated and the remaining battery capacity is estimated. Moreover, their Petri net model was further applied to the design and evaluation of several dynamic power management solutions [11]. Based on Petri nets, Shareef *et al.* [12] also developed a model of a wireless sensor node that can accurately estimate the energy consumption. They used this model to identify an optimal threshold for powering down a sensor node of a specific wireless sensor application.

Most of the previous work focused on developing a conceptual sensor model and provided limited results on realistic measurement or comparative experiments. By applying our previously proposed Petri net framework in [13], this work has modeled the energy consumption of a ZigBee-equipped sensor node. Furthermore, an experiment has been conducted to measure the real power consumption and provide input parameters to the PN model, which could be applied to further simulations of ZigBee-based WSNs. This is the sense to use the PN model to describe the power consumption of sensor nodes.

The rest of this paper is organized as follows. Section II introduces the Petri net model of a wireless sensor. Then, experimental results are provided in Section III. Finally, Section IV concludes this paper.

II. Petri Net Modeling of Wireless Sensors

This section will introduce the MultiParadigm Modeling (MPaM) methodology, and then show the behavior modeling of networked wireless sensors.

A. *MultiParadigm Modeling (MPaM)*

To deal with specific and complicated problems, we have to integrate heterogeneous modeling arts, thereby resulting in the MPaM methodology. It is based on a proposition of giving different entities of a complex system the most appropriate modeling abstractions [13]. From a viewpoint of MPaM, the PN is adopted to design and analyze coordination controllers in a discrete-event domain. The primary motivation for employing PN as hybrid models is the situation that all those good characteristics that make discrete PN a valuable discrete-event model still be available to hybrid systems. Examples of these characteristics include: PN does not need the exhaustive enumeration of the state space at the design stage and can finitely model systems with an infinite state space. Moreover, PN provides a modular description where the structure of each module is maintained in the composed model. Furthermore, discrete states of PN are modeled by a vector and not by a symbolic label, thus linear algebraic techniques may be adopted for system analysis.

Figure 1 represents the previously proposed PN framework for modeling a system in discrete-event and discrete-time domains [13]. Each operation is modeled with a *command* transition to start the operation, a progressive *working* place, a *response* transition to end the operation, and a *completed* place. Note that the start transition (drawn with a dark symbol) is a controllable event as "command" input, while the end transition is an uncontrollable event as "response" output. The working place is a Hierarchical Hybrid Place (HHP, drawn with a triple circle), in which the state equations of the systems to be controlled are contained and interacted through the boundary interface. The interaction between event-driven and time-driven domains is realized in the following way: a token put into the working place triggers a discrete (or continuous) time process with the corresponding equations. Thresholds are monitored concurrently. Each threshold is corresponding to a transition, that is, the response transitions. When the threshold is reached or crossed, it indicates that the associated event is happening, and the corresponding transition is fired. Next, a new marking is evaluated, and the combination of the hybrid system restarts.

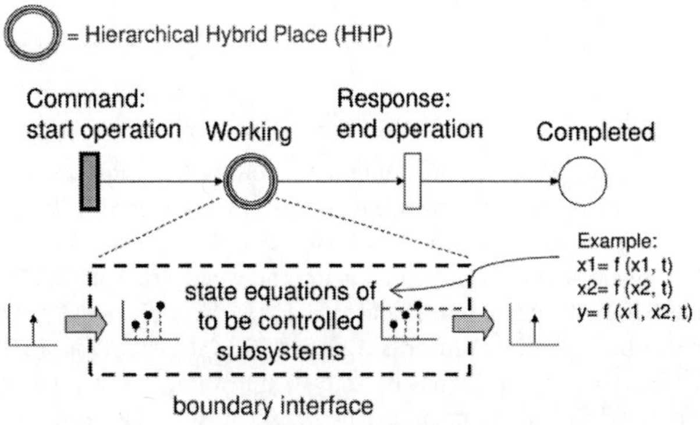

Figure 1. Multiparadigm modeling within a Petri net framework [13].

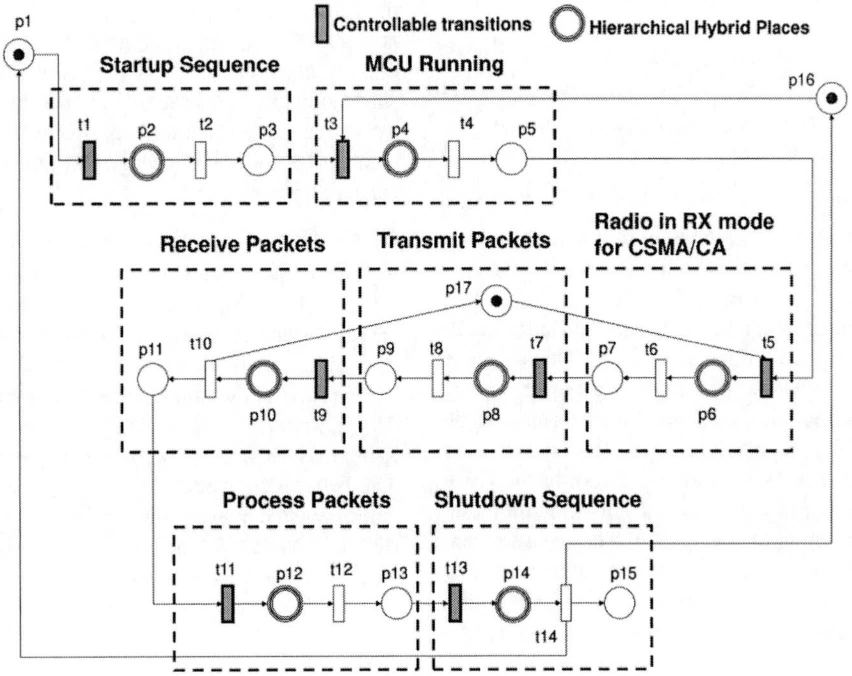

Figure 2. Petri net model of a networked wireless sensor.

TABLE I.
NOTATION FOR PETRI NET OF A WIRELESS SENSOR IN FIGURE 1

Place	Description	Transition	Description
p1	Node in sleep mode	t1	Cmd: start startup sequence
p2	MCU running at 16MHz	t2	Re: end startup sequence
p3	Startup sequence completed	t3	Cmd: start running MCU at 32MHz
p4	MCU running at 32MHz	t4	Re: end running MCU
p5	MCU running completed	t5	Cmd: start CSMA/CA operation
p6	Radio in RX mode	t6	Re: end CSMA/CA operation
p7	CSMA/CA operation completed	t7	Cmd: start transmitting packets
p8	Radio in TX mode	t8	Re: end transmitting packets
p9	Packet transmission completed	t9	Cmd: start receiving packets
p10	Radio in RX mode	t10	Re: end receiving packets
p11	Packet reception completed	t11	Cmd: start processing packets
p12	Processing packets	t12	Re: end processing packets
p13	Processing packets completed	t13	Cmd: start shutdown sequence
p14	MCU running at 16MHz	t14	Re: end shutdown sequence
p15	Shutdown sequence completed		
p16	MCU is available		
p17	Radio is available		

B. *Behavior Modeling of Networked Wireless Sensors*

In general, the radio communication is the most energy consuming part of a wireless sensor as compared with its sensing and computation tasks. Hence, our model focuses on the operations of packet transmission and reception. By applying the design procedure in [13], the PN model of a networked wireless sensor is constructed as shown in Figure 2, which consists of 17 places and 14 transitions, respectively. The corresponding notations are described in Table I. The model is based on a scenario where a sensor node periodically transmits and receives some data towards, for example, a base station.

III. EXPERIMENT AND RESULTS

This section will firstly show the measurement setup and experimental results. Then, the comparisons between the measurement and PN model will be described.

A. *Measurement Setup*

In this section, the energy consumption of a wireless sensor as computed via its Petri net model will be compared against real measurements collected from a ZigBee-equipped sensor node. The measurement setup in [14] has been adopted as shown in Figure 3 (a), in which a ZigBee End Device is the Device Under Test (DUT) and powered by a power supply. The energy consumption measurements are performed at the End Device, which periodically (every 0.5 sec in our measurement) wakes up and sends data to the coordinator (base station). The voltage across a 10 Ohm resistor is monitored to determine the current draw of the system. The measurement system has been calibrated with both a digital oscilloscope and a digital multimeter to ensure an accurate measurement. Figure 3 (b) shows the hardware setup during energy consumption measurement.

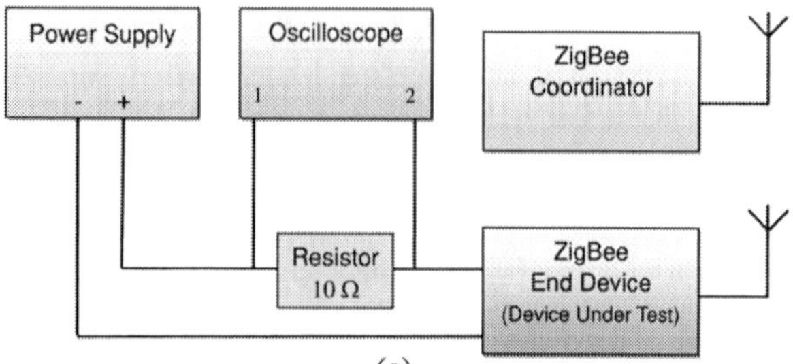

(a)

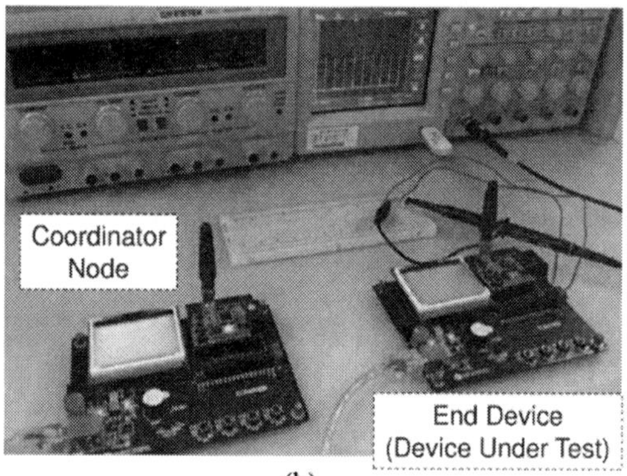

(b)

Figure 3. (a) Measurement configuration and (b) hardware setup during energy consumption measurement.

B. *Measurement Results*

Figure 4 (a) shows the power consumption during sleep and awake states. The time base on the oscilloscope is set to 500 ms per division, and it can be seen that it is about 0.5 sec among each current peak, showing the power consumption when the device is awake to send the data to the coordinator. Figure 4 (b) is a zoomed version of Figure 4 (a) and shows the current consumption during the active modes in more details. This snapshot has a time base of 1 ms per division. The duration of the active mode is about 7 ms. According to the measurement results, the consumed energy and duration of each operation can be estimated.

C. *Comparisons between Measurement and Petri Net Model*

With the measured sets of consumed current and duration for each transition as the inputs to the Petri net model, the energy consumption can be obtained as shown in Figure 5. In general, the energy consumption of the Petri net model is close to the practical measurement with a mean difference of around 0.9%. However, several peak currents appear during the state transitions, especially the startup sequence t1. Moreover, note that between transitions t7 and t9, there are two V-shaped gullies, which present the transceiver turnaround operations (RX to TX and TX to RX). Future work would attempt to model such detailed behaviors.

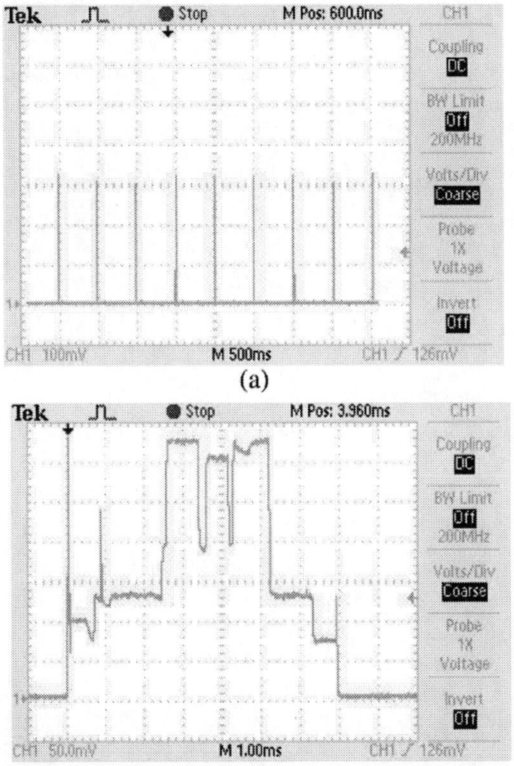

(b)

Figure 4. Measurement results for the division scale at (a) 500 ms and (b) 1 ms.

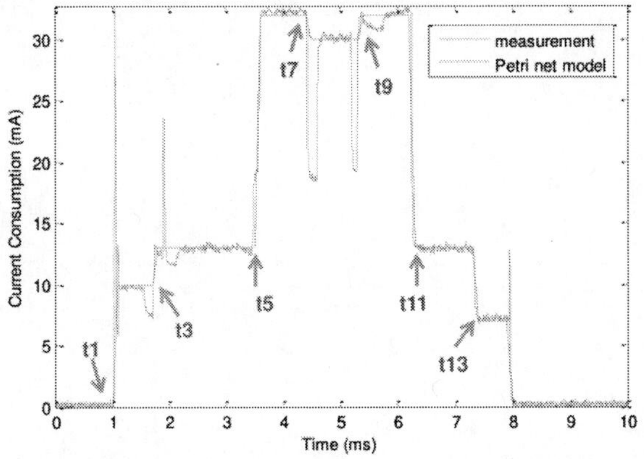

Figure 5. Comparison of energy consumption between measurement and Petri net model.

Obviously, the description of the power consumption of a single node during a standard RX/TX procedure is a very isolated scenario. For example, the power consumption of a node would significantly change when a collision is happening during transmission with a subsequent packet loss which requires a repeated transmission. Future work would consider more practical interactions between the nodes so as to simulate the power consumption of a whole sensor network for different scenarios.

IV. CONCLUSION AND FUTURE WORK

In this paper, a systematic approach to modeling and measurement of energy consumption for wireless sensors has been presented. The sensor operation is modeled using the Petri nets. Then, an experiment has been conducted to measure the real power consumption and provide input parameters to the Petri net model. The comparative results indicate the Petri net model has approximated the real measurement under the assumed scenarios. Besides the periodical operations demonstrated in this paper, the measurement scheme is also useful for other specific applications and could be fed back to the Petri net model as a calibration source.

Since the proposed Petri net model in this paper is mainly designed for packet transmission and reception, as a future work, operations of sensing and computation tasks could be further considered so as to make the model much more realistic. Moreover, with a given battery, the proposed model could be further applied to the lifetime estimation for periodical operations.

ACKNOWLEDGMENT

This paper was supported by the Ministry of Science and Technology (MOST) of Taiwan under grant MOST-106-2221-E-027-057.

The authors would like to thank Mr. Yu-Kai Wang from Information & Communications Research Labs, Industrial Technology Research Institute (ITRI) for his help with the experiment.

REFERENCES

[1] J. S. Lee and Y. C. Lee, "An application of grey prediction to transmission power control in mobile sensor networks," *IEEE Internet of Things J.*, vol. 5, no. 3, pp. 2154-2162, Jun. 2018.

[2] W. Q. Guo, W. M. Healy, and M. C. Zhou, "Impacts of 2.4-GHz ISM band interference on IEEE 802.15.4 wireless sensor network reliability in buildings," *IEEE Trans. Instrum. Meas.*, vol. 61, no. 9, pp. 2533-2544, Sep. 2012.

[3] J. S. Lee and W. L. Cheng, "A fuzzy-logic-based clustering approach for wireless sensor networks using energy predication," *IEEE Sensors J.*, vol. 12, no. 9, pp. 2891-2897, Sep. 2012.

[4] J. S. Lee, "A Petri net design of command filters for semi-autonomous mobile sensor networks," *IEEE Trans. Ind. Electron.*, vol. 55, no. 4, pp. 1835-1841, Apr. 2008.

[5] G. Anastasi, M. Conti, M. D. Francesco, and A. Passarella, "Energy conservation in wireless sensor networks: A survey," *Ad Hoc Netw.*, vol. 7, no. 3, pp. 537-568, May 2009.

[6] J. S. Lee and T. Y. Kao, "An improved three-layer low-energy adaptive clustering hierarchy for wireless sensor networks," *IEEE Internet of Things J.*, vol. 3, no. 6, pp. 951-958, Dec. 2016.

[7] J. S. Lee and C. L. Teng, "An enhanced hierarchical clustering approach for mobile sensor networks using fuzzy inference systems," *IEEE Internet of Things J.*, vol. 4, no. 4, pp. 1095-1103, Aug. 2017.

[8] B. Bougard, F. Catthoor, D. C. Daly, A. Chandrakasan, and W. Dehaene, "Energy efficiency of the IEEE 802.15.4 standard in dense wireless microsensor networks: Modeling and improvement perspectives," in *Proc. of Design, Automation and Test in Europe Conference and Exhibition (DATE)*, Munich, Germany, Mar. 2005, pp. 196-201.

[9] M. C. Ekstrom, M. Bergblomma, M. Linden, M. Bjorkman, and M. Ekstrom, "A Bluetooth radio energy consumption model for low-duty-cycle applications," *IEEE Trans. Instrum. Meas.*, vol. 61, no. 3, pp. 609-617, Mar. 2012.

[10] J. R. B. Sousa, A. M. N. Lima, and A. Perkusich, "Modeling and analyzing power consumption in sensor networks nodes based on differential hybrid

Petri nets," in *Proc. The Annual Conf. IEEE Industrial Electronics Society (IECON)*, Raleigh, NC, Nov. 2005, pp. 389-394.

[11] P. S. Sausen, J. R. B. Sousa, M. A. Spohn, A. Perkusich, and A. M. N. Lima, "Dynamic power management with scheduled switching modes," *Comput. Commun.*, vol. 31, pp. 3625-3637, Sep. 2008.

[12] A. Shareef and Y. F. Zhu, "Power modeling of wireless sensor nodes based on Petri net," in *Proc. The 39th Int. Conf. Parallel Processing*, San Diego, CA, Sep. 2010, pp. 101-110.

[13] J. S. Lee, M. C. Zhou, and P. L. Hsu, "Multiparadigm modeling for hybrid dynamic systems using a Petri net framework," *IEEE Trans. Syst., Man, Cybern. A, Syst., Humans*, vol. 38, no. 2, pp. 493-498, Mar. 2008.

[14] B. Selvig, "Measuring power consumption with CC2430 & Z-Stack," Application Note AN053, Texas Instruments. Jul. 2007.